TALES
—— OF ——
BIALYSTOK

A Jewish Journey from Czarist Russia to America

TALES

—OF—

BIALYSTOK

A Jewish Journey from Czarist Russia to America

CHARLES ZACHARIAH GOLDBERG
Translated from the Yiddish by
Phyllis Goldberg Ross

Rootstock Publishing

First Printing: November 15, 2017

Tales of Bialystok: A Jewish Journey from Czarist Russia to America
Copyright © 2017 by Phyllis Goldberg Ross
All Rights Reserved.

ISBN-10: 1578690048
ISBN-13: 9781578690046
Library of Congress Control Number: 2017942822

Published by Rootstock Publishing
www.rootstockpublishing.com
An imprint of Multicultural Media Inc.
info@rootstockpublishing.com

Front Cover Design by Stephen McArthur
Book Design by Carrie Cook

Printed in the USA

DEDICATION

*To my father, Charles (Zachariah) Goldberg,
of blessed memory, and to his descendants with the
hope that his words will be meaningful to them
and help them to appreciate a very special man.*

*The Goldberg Family from Menkhes Street, left to right, Reb Isaac,
the cantor; his children Beilke, Daniel, who was mayor of Colchester CT,
Charles Zacariah, their mother Keyle, and daughter Sheinke.*

Charlie as a young man in America.

THE MAGIC OF THE WRITTEN WORD

A Foreword from the Translator

My father, who died in 1954, never had much formal education. He was born in Bialystok, Poland and came to the United States in 1906 at the age of 17 after a devastating pogrom in his hometown. From time to time after his arrival in America he wrote letters to the editors of some of the New York Yiddish-language newspapers; those that were published, he cut out and pasted in a notebook. In the 1940s, my father started to write what he called "episodes" from his youth. Many of these stories were published in Yiddish newspapers and in the *Voice of Bialystok*, the journal of his landsmen's society. I knew he kept a notebook of these clippings, but he never spoke about them. Since they were all in Yiddish I had no idea what was in them. He died in 1954 and my mother kept the notebook until she died in 1982. In looking through my mother's things, I found the notebook; in all the years since her death I never even opened it.

At the turn of the millennium, I suddenly decided it was time; these stories could be a legacy for future generations. The only problem was that, although I could speak Yiddish, I couldn't read it. Yiddish is written using Hebrew letters. I knew the Hebrew alphabet, and little by little I taught myself to read Yiddish and began translating the "episodes" into English. The results were incredible. I learned things about my father's life that he had never spoken of: How he had been apprenticed to a furniture maker for three years beginning at the age of eleven with only bed and board as his wages;

at the end of three years, his parents were paid 20 rubles. What it was like studying with a cruel teacher in a Talmud Torah in Russia before the turn of the 20th century. How he had barely escaped a group of marauding Cossacks. How he had fled Czarist Russia by traveling at night from safe house to safe house via a kind of "underground railroad," and many other fascinating, often sad, experiences. He also related stories about events that he had not experienced but were told to him and obviously made a significant impression on him. Because my father committed his thoughts to paper, I have found out things in my father's life that would have been lost forever, and can share them with others.

– *Phyllis Goldberg Ross*
August 2017

Special thanks to Kenneth Newman, Ellen Ross-Newman, Rhoda Carroll, and Tim Joslyn without whose assistance this project could not have been completed.

A note from the translator: The Yiddish word for czar was pronounced as tsar, which means "trouble, woe." The Russian ruler was certainly the source of a great deal of pain and suffering for the Jews of Russia at that time. It's a word play which doesn't come through in the translation.

*From a Painting of oldest Jewish
street in Bialystok.*

*Count Jan Klemens Branicki II
(1689-1771) The owner of Bialystok,
gift of the Czar.*

The old Jewish cemetery 1917, now disappeared.

The Pale

0   500 km

Baltic Sea

Prussia

Moscow

Dvinsk
Vitebsk
Smolensk
Kovno
Vilno
Suwalki
Minsk
Mogilev
Grodno
Bobruysk
Plock
Lomza Bialystok
Gomel
Siedlice
Warsaw
Kalisz
Lodz
Pinsk
Piotrkow
Brest-Litovsk
Radom
Chernigov
Kielce
Lublin
Zhitomir
Kiev
Poltava
Berdichev
Kremenchug
Kamenets-Podolsky
Elizavetgrad
Ekaterinoslav

Austria-Hungary

Kherson
Odessa
Kishinev

Simferopol

Romania

Black Sea

Russia

TABLE OF CONTENTS

In front of the Jewish hospital, in the aftermath of the
June 1906 Bialystok pogrom.

IN THE SHADOW OF DEATH

This happened in the year 1906, in the time when waves of pogroms spread over cities and towns all over Russia, and Jewish blood poured out like water, including in the city of Bialystok. Several weeks beforehand we already knew that the local regime had decided that our city would have a pogrom. We heard the information from the Jewish soldiers who were serving in the city militia.

The young Jewish men decided to set up a self-defense organization, and as a young man myself then, I also joined the group. Feverish activity began. We drilled and were assigned various responsibilities; we prepared ourselves exactly as if for a war. Naturally, everything was done in strict secrecy.

The day came that had been designated in advance for the pogrom. From quite early on a lot of restlessness could be detected among the peasants. There was a lot of commotion in the marketplace; the air seemed filled with gunpowder. The shops were closed. Very few Jews showed themselves in the street. And if a Jew was seen, he was running and not walking. One could read the fright on every Jewish face.

Eleven o'clock. The self-defense group sends out patrols. At exactly twelve o'clock a religious procession is supposed to pass by. That is to be the signal to begin the slaughter. And now the lonely tolling of the town clock is heard. Each clang is a monotone: one, two, three—and so on until twelve.

In the distance the procession can be seen. Priests march in front, carrying holy images, and behind them is a crowd numbering in the thousands. The streets are heavily guarded by police and soldiers.

Everything seems calm. The thought begins to cross my mind that perhaps all the fear is for nothing. But suddenly a terrific explosion is heard. The very air shudders. It is a bomb, the provocation that is the herald for the slaughter. People run around, shooting begins, and bullets fly overhead.

I run from a patrol to a central meeting place to join the other comrades from the self-help group. As I run I feel as if my feet don't even come near the ground. Bullets fall around me. Who knows if I will arrive safely at the prearranged rendezvous. Suddenly I see in the distance a Cossack patrol coming towards me. Continuing to run means going directly into the hands of the Cossacks. I approach the closest door. The door is shut tight. I shove with all my strength and the door opens. I run quickly into the courtyard; I want to push the door closed, but it is already too late.

The sound of hoofbeats gets closer. I squeeze into a little corner between the stalls under a mountainous woodpile. Quickly I creep in between the logs; I cover myself with wood all around. I hold my breath; I'm afraid to breathe. Lying like that for a few minutes, I hear that the Cossacks are already in the courtyard. They are searching and rummaging in every little corner. (What I lived through then is dreadful even now as I recall it.) Through something like a miracle they don't look through this pile of wood. They remount their horses and dash off at a gallop. A cold sweat pours over me. I remain there until it gets a little quieter and I drag myself to the meeting place of the self-help group.

*Memorial to victims
of 1906 Pogrom.*

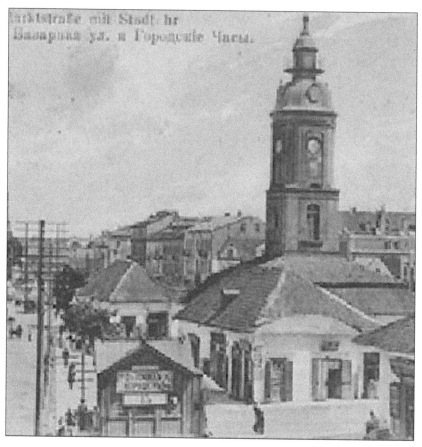

"And now the lonely tolling of the town clock is heard.
Each clang is a monotone: one, two, three—and so on until twelve."

LIFE EXPERIENCES

This happened to me when I was still "green," the first year in this country. Arriving in New York City as a furniture maker from the old country, I got my first job in a furniture factory. I found out at once that all eight workers were Germans. Apparently, even then, forty years ago, Germans didn't exactly love Jews, especially "green" ones. It seems as though they had decided among themselves to harass the newcomer to death. And I must mention here that they were, to a degree, successful. They simply made my life miserable. I thought many times of leaving the job, but how could I find another, even for such pitiful wages as six dollars a week?

So I suffered in silence. When they saw that they couldn't even get rid of me with practical jokes, they began to torment me physically. As soon as they noticed that I was concentrating on my work, I would feel something fly at my head. I'd ask them to leave me alone; they would laugh at me. Bit by bit I began to feel bitterness in my heart. However, I was helpless. It didn't help when I complained to the boss; it made my ordeal even worse. I continued to suffer in silence and hoped a time would come when I could avenge myself for my suffering.

One day, one of the workers asked me to crawl under the workbench and bring out a certain tool. Suspecting nothing, I

crawled under the workbench to reach the tool. Suddenly I felt a
terrible blow to my body. Things got black before my eyes. I thought
that the whole building had fallen in on me. Barely able to crawl
out from under the workbench, I was writhing in pain. I asked my
tormentors to call an ambulance because I was sure that some of my
bones were broken. They laughed heartily at me and said, *"Der Yude
shtarbt nicht so schnel!"* ("A Jew doesn't die so quickly!") I wanted to
grab a piece of wood and fight them, ready to die at the hands of
the Philistines, but I could hardly move from pain.

I managed to drag myself home to my lodgings where I
remained in bed several days. When I felt better, I went back to the
factory. During the time I was in bed, one thought tormented me...
how to avenge myself on those damned Germans.

I didn't have to wait long. In the factory was what we called a
"steam table," where wood was dried before use. It was the custom
for everyone to sit around this table to eat lunch. I sat down as well
and unwrapped my meager lunch, which consisted of a few pieces
of bread and a can of sardines. I bent over to pick up of a bit of
wood from the floor to pry open the can of sardines, as was then the
custom among woodworkers. When I raised my head, neither bread
nor sardines were there. I asked them to return my lunch, but they
just laughed at me. There was no time left to go elsewhere and buy
another lunch because very soon the whistle would blow and we
would have to go back to work. And I was famished.

The blood rushed to my head; I became like a wild animal.
All the bitterness that had accumulated over time suddenly
exploded. I grabbed a piece of wood and began knocking their
lunch boxes off the table. In one minute, all their lunches lay on the

floor. For a moment they sat there, stunned. When they recovered their wits, all eight threw themselves at me. I started swinging left and right with the piece of wood; one after another they fell down bloodied. True, I was young and strong then, but how I managed to accomplish this I do not understand to this day.

In the commotion, I escaped from the factory, leaving them lying bloody on the floor. I went back to my lodgings and told the landlady that I was not coming home for several days until everything quieted down. A week later I returned to my lodgings. Nobody had been there looking for me.

*Fontanna, the central fountain where unemployed
Jews and Christian men waited for jobs.*

MEMORIES OF MENKHES GESEL

Since in the last issue of the *Shtime* were several articles about old Bialystok, I would like (although I'm no writer), as much as my poor pen will allow, to tell about my beloved Bialystok. I will not write about the Bialystok of the great factories and wealthy businesses. Nor about Navelifeh or Veshlikaveh Streets with their wealthy shops. Several others have already done this, and better writers at that. Here I will write about a little street in Bialystok that most Bialystokers knew little of.

Who among you remembers Menkhes Gesel (street)? Yes, that's where I was born. My cradle used to stand in Lazer's courtyard in one of the poor little houses. That's where I spent my childhood, played with the other little boys, there experienced my entire youth until, three days after the pogrom of 1906, I went away to America. My father (may he rest in peace) was a poor weaver, worked for Zelig Yashinovski, and later for Leybl Mavshovski. I used to see my father very seldom. He worked from early in the morning until late at night. And from those long and difficult hours he barely eked out a living. And my mother had to spin yarn and do other work in order to help earn enough so we would not suffer from hunger. My Menkhes Gesel with its poor little houses stands before my eyes now, forty years later. I believe that I would still be able to recognize every little stone of its broken cobblestone pavement.

There were no wealthy people in our little street. We didn't have any Mordechai Gordons or Leon Zackheims. Most of the men and boys were poor artisans. I will try to describe one of them. He was called Reb Leyb. He was a cobbler, a poor Jew who made his living from putting a patch on a torn shoe. He never complained about his fate and was a very cheerful soul. To make jokes and play tricks was a pleasure to him. And when Erev Shabbos (the eve of the Sabbath)or Erev Yom Tov (eve of a holiday) came and his wife,Khasa Malka, asked him for money to buy something in the market, Reb Leyb, not getting up from the cobbler's bench, would mutter into his beard: "Don't worry yourself so. The Master of the World who feeds a little worm in the earth will also not abandon us."

One time it was close to Pesach (Passover.) Malka was pacing around the house and said to Leyb, "What will happen? It's almost Pesach already and there's no sign of matzah, or eggs, or wine that we need for Pesach." And Leyb, according to his nature, turned his head and said to her, "Malka, don't worry. We'll have Pesach just like all the Jews." Soon it was Erev Pesach in the morning. Jews got up early and hurried to the synagogue to pray and to observe the Fast of Bekorim. Reb Leyb was seen wandering around outside hither and yon and from his eyes poured tears. "What happened, Reb Leyb?" asked the neighbors. And Reb Leyb related that a tragedy had befallen him the previous night. Someone had stolen his entire Pesach. The matzah, the wine, the eggs, and the shmaltz (chicken fat)... all were stolen. "What will I do now?" he said. The Jews, having pity on him, comforted him. "Don't worry, Reb Leyb, you'll have everything you need for Pesach." And it didn't take long for the women to begin to bring everything that was needed: matzah, eggs, shmaltz, and enough wine for four cups. And Reb Leyb had a good Pesach. Right after Pesach Reb Leyb told the truth, that the night before Pesach he was not robbed. Because there was nothing to steal. So what happened? He saw that it was already Erev Pesach and not a groshen was in the house, and this was the only remedy so that they would not be hungry on Pesach.

And here is another Jew from our little street, the Yeshinovker, he was called, a teacher of the youngest Jewish children. A small, thin man who taught little ones the alphabet. As short as he was in stature, so great was his soul. A good-natured man.

And not far away was the Shereshaver teacher, a tall Jew with stern eyes, a very irascible man. He taught Rashi and Pentateuch to the young boys. And if a father said to his young son that this time he was going to the Shereshaver's *kheder (Hebrew school)*, the boy would be terrified because the teacher beat the students.

And here is another rabbi of mine, Reb Mordechai Aharon, teacher of *Gemara, (a rabbinical commentary)*, a Jew of stately appearance. He put his whole life into his students so that something would become of them. Every page of *Gemara* that he studied with his students remained with them forever. We loved him with all our hearts and souls. He never laid a hand on any student. Always with kindness.

And who can forget Reb Motel Vasserfierer at the corner of Menkhes and Shmuel Shmids Streets? A Jew who considered himself one of the well-to-do, he had a grocery. He sold water by the bucket. In his house was a kettle with hot water that was always

11

simmering and he would sell a glass of tea for a groshen or a kopek. He also kept a few cows to provide the poor people with a bit of milk to whiten up their barley soup. He was the rich man of our little street.

I also remember Reb T'nachum Beker. A tall Jew with broad shoulders, a mighty man. It was said of him that he would wrestle in the circus with the professional strongmen. He had a bagel bakery. Always standing in a pit near the burning oven, he shaped each bagel on a stick and then threw it into the pot of boiling water, cooked the bagel, and then took it out with the same stick. He then placed it on a large, flat paddle, made sure the bagel was nice and circular, and put it into the oven. What beautiful, browned bagels came from his hands, what delicious bagels those were. Even now the taste lingers in my mouth.

In the same courtyard was the Grodner bagel maker, a Jew who knew the *shvartze pintelakh* (fine points of Jewish learning) but who did not engage in the baking. He always went about with his hands behind him, humming a little *nigun* (melody) from the *Gemarah,* never a loud word was ever heard from his mouth. The one who ran the bakery was his son-in-law, Nissen. A sturdily built young man, he kneaded the dough and baked the bagels; he was a hard worker.

Across the way was Abraham, the Hebrew teacher. He taught young boys and girls grammar. In the evening he hurried about giving private lessons. And there was Moshe-Nachum, a stitcher, a Jew who was by no means a scholar. He supported the shoemakers' *shul* (synagogue) with wood and gas for the lamps. His payment for that was the pulpit. For a *kabalat shabbat,* (ushering in the Sabbath) he provided a measure of wood. As for the pious man who devoted himself exclusively to the study of the sacred books and who sat in the shoemakers' House of Study day and night, no one could find out where he came from. He lived on bread and water. When the women brought him some cooked food, that was fine; if not, a dry piece of bread was enough. One beautiful morning they found him dead. In his pockets they found a piece of paper that stated that the only thing he wanted was that someone would say *Kaddish* (the prayer for the dead) for him and would observe the anniversary of his death.

And who from our little street does not remember the Karliner house of worship above the shoemakers' house of study. The evening meal ushering out the Sabbath and observation of the anniversaries of deaths were observed there. What bliss the Chassidim enjoyed from a small glass of shnaps. Such fiery Chassidim as Yehoshe Hillel, the synagogue warden from the voluntary committee and Mordechai Itche, the weaver, and other such Chassidim drowned their poverty in a glass of whiskey and dined on a little dancing.

I will never forget how one *Simchas Torah (the holiday marking the end of the annual cycle of public Torah readings and the beginning of a new cycle)* the cantor was standing near the lectern and singing all kinds of melodies as is the custom for this holiday. Fellow Chassidim brought in a tub of water and placed it behind the cantor. When the cantor was at the point of singing *Osey Shalom,* he stepped back a few steps and fell into the tub of water. Do you think, Heaven forbid, that he became angry? No. The water ran from him and, soaking wet, he joined in with the other Chassidim in a dance, and the sounds of the dancers rose to Heaven itself. And when a "real" Rabbi once came there on a Shabbos, don't even ask about what excitement went on in the house of prayer.

In such an atmosphere did I spend my youth. Is it then any wonder that Bialystok lies deep in my heart? All the years that I've spent in America I hoped that a time would come when I would again be able to step on the ground of Bialystok. Now I know that my sweet dream will never come true. My native city lies in ruins. Every little stone is soaked in the blood of my family and friends, destroyed in violent deaths, burned in the ovens, buried alive. The murderous Nazis exceeded with their cruelty all the Hamens of diaspora history.

May their bones be cursed for ten generations. May Jewish blood not be silent like the prophet Zakharia's was not silent. May they be erased from this earth.

THE INFORMER

The Czarist government ordered that, during periods of military conscription, each community had to provide a specific number of recruits. In those days Jews didn't have much enthusiasm for serving in the Russian army because of the brutal laws that were directed toward them and made their daily lives very difficult. Confined to the Pale of Settlement, the Jews were simply being suffocated. It was no wonder that men sought a variety of means to avoid serving in the military. The sons of the rich were either exempted from service or paid dearly for their freedom. For poor boys, the only solution was to inflict an injury that would make them ineligible for the army.

In those days there were people who were called *makhers*. For the right price, they would cause an appropriate injury. Sometimes the *makhers* would cause deafness or would pour drops in the eyes. Sometimes, they would even chop off a finger. Another way was for the young men to make themselves ill by not eating or sleeping and losing a lot of weight. When they appeared for induction, they could barely stand on their feet. That was about the only way a poor man's son could avoid the army.

When the Russians realized that the Jews were not providing enough recruits, and indeed those who did appear for induction were mostly cripples, the government issued a decree that young boys were to be taken to fill the quota. When the order became known, it was as shocking as thunder booming out of a clear sky. Despair gripped the entire Jewish population; they knew that a great tragedy was about to befall them.

The edict contained two elements: first, the quota had to be filled with young boys, and second, they were to be transported deep into Russia, into villages and hamlets so that in time they would forget their origins and could be converted to the Greek Orthodox faith. This religion would gain many thousand converts, for it was always an important goal of theirs to entrap Jewish souls.

As the time of the conscription would draw near, the entire Jewish community would be in terrible turmoil. Mothers and fathers didn't know what to do with their young sons... how to hide them. While some solution might have been found to deal with these circumstances, a new disaster occurred... the Jewish *khapers* (kidnappers). The Russian government paid them to reveal in which homes young boys could be found. To our great shame, they performed their task perfectly. The tears and shrieks of the wretched parents whose children were taken away reached the very heavens. More than one mother fell dead at the kidnappers' feet when they dragged her *kaddish* (eldest son) out of her arms.

One of these kidnappers who lived in our town was named Berele. He had no significant livelihood, so when kidnapping children turned out to be a good way of earning a living, he became one of them. And it soon became clear what kind of black soul he had. No one could hide from Berele; no one could squirm out of his hands. In a word, he became the terror of the entire town.

When the Jews saw that this evildoer was destroying the town, several respected men went to the rabbi to ask him to do something about this situation. The rabbi at that time was Reb Velvel, a highly esteemed individual whose piety was without limit. He was one of those old-fashioned rabbis who knew but one thing: to study Torah constantly. He was truly a singular man in his generation.

When Reb Velvel heard what was going on, he immediately called over the *shamash* (sexton) and told him to bring Berele. When the *shamash* told Berele that the rabbi wanted to see him, Berele laughed in his face. When the *shamash* returned to the rabbi with Berele's answer, the rabbi replied: "Go tell Berele that he must come... the request has the force of an official religious decree."

Once again the *shamash* went to Berele and repeated the rabbi's words. Berele violently berated the *shamash* and denounced the rabbi in highly inappropriate language. He also made it clear that he was going to continue with his "work."

When the *shamash* returned a second time to the rabbi to deliver Berele's answer, Reb Velvel put his head between his hands and fell into deep concentration about how to deal with this matter. Suddenly, as if awakening from a trance, he decided to address the *balebatim* (upstanding men) of the community.

"If the villain will not come voluntarily, he'll come against his will. This is what you must do. Trick him into meeting with you on a secluded street. Pretend you want to talk business with him. And when you succeed in persuading him to accompany you, be sure to pass by my window. I simply want to look at him."

When they were able to persuade Berele to agree to the meeting, the rabbi was told that he was on his way. The rabbi approached his window, raised bushy eyebrows that almost hid his eyes, and stared for a long time at the face of the betrayer of Israel. He then moved away from the window and returned to his study of the *Gemara* as if nothing had happened.

As the informer passed a few feet from the rabbi's house, he suddenly fell down in the middle of the street. A great tumult arose and people flocked to the site. The police arrived and brought a doctor, but Berele was dead. And as befitted a man like Berele, he was buried beyond the cemetery fence like an animal, and the town rejoiced.

MY FATHER'S ADVICE

This incident happened to me forty years ago. When I first came to this country from home, it was not difficult for me to find work because I was a skilled craftsman, a carpenter. I went to work in a factory, but the work was not congenial. I simply could not get accustomed to the situation that existed in factories in those days. One has to earn a living, however, so I worked and hoped that the time would come when I would be able to extricate myself from the factory. After working in the factory for a while, I got the opportunity.

At that time my brother was planning to emigrate from Europe. Being a butcher by trade, he got a job in a small town in Connecticut through an ad in the "Morgen Journal." After spending some time in that community with the butcher and familiarizing himself with the town, he saw an opportunity to go into business for himself. One day I received a letter from my brother letting me know of his decision. He also wrote me that if I wanted, I could go there, too, and we would become partners. Since I was looking for an opportunity to get away from the factory, I quickly packed my bundle and went to him. We opened a butcher shop, and with time would have made a good living and had a good future. However, it didn't take long for me to realize that I couldn't get along with my brother in business. I decided to dissolve the partnership and do something on my own.

It so happened that the opportunity arose to go into the boardinghouse business. I rented a farmhouse not far from town, and since it was already after Pesach (Passover), I set to work to put everything in order so that when the 'season' would come I would be ready for business. All day long I would spend at the farm engaged in various activities, and when it began to get dark, would go into town to my night's lodging. I didn't want to sleep alone in the farmhouse not because I was afraid, but because it isn't good for a person to sleep alone on an isolated farm. After all, a person is merely a person; who knows what might happen. It's better to be among people.

On a certain evening when I came to the people with whom I was lodging, I was told that family was coming from New York to visit and they would be staying the night. I would have to give up my bed for the guests. I could have found lodging with someone else for the night, but I didn't want to inconvenience anyone, so I decided to go back to the farm to sleep. I passed time in town until eleven o'clock and then set out for the farm.

After I'd gone about half way, the skies suddenly clouded over and in a few brief minutes a terrible storm broke out. A downpour like a flood spilled down, accompanied by dreadful thunder and lightning. Here I am, half way between the town and the farm. There is no place to shelter from the rain. With every minute I become more drenched by the rain. What should I do? Going back to town is just as far as going to the farm. And the storm is getting stronger; it's as if the flood gates of heaven opened up. I must quickly decide what to do; without pondering too much, I decide to go to the farm.

I hasten my pace and find myself near the cemetery that is midway between town and the farm and which I must pass. The lightning and thunder continue. A sudden flash of lightning illuminates the entire area as if it were midday. The awareness that I am near the cemetery creeps into my head. I become a little disturbed but try to drive away the gloom thoughts. There is a terrible flash of lightning; involuntarily I glance toward the cemetery. In the illumination of the lightning flash I think I see a silhouette among the gravestones.

Although I am not by nature a coward, I nevertheless become frightened and try to hurry my steps. But my feet won't move. I force myself to go a little further on, regretting that I didn't decide to return to town. But it's a lost cause; it's too late now to go back.

Another bolt of bright lightning flashes and the cemetery is illuminated. I can now clearly see that among the gravestones stands a person dressed in white, moving his arms back and forth. I do not understand what is happening, because I know that the dead do not rise out of their graves, yet here I clearly see someone dressed in white.

This is getting to be a bit too much for my nerves. But at that moment I recall that my father, may he rest in peace, used to always tell me that if you are frightened by something, you dare not leave the place until you find out what it is. I realize that if I don't want to be forever under the impression that I have seen a ghost, I must immediately investigate. I don't think about it too long. I cross the road and stand at the cemetery fence waiting for another flash of lightning so that I can see if it is really a ghost. I don't have to wait long. Once again a lightning bolt flashes and in its light I see what frightened me. Draped over a tombstone is a white shirt that must have been blown off someone's laundry line by the wind. It had caught on a tombstone and since the sleeves were free and the wind was blowing, the sleeves flapped back and forth. From a distance it looked like a person standing among the gravestones and waving.

I calmed down and in my heart thanked my father for the good advice that if something frightens you, you should investigate it. If I hadn't done that, all my life I would have been under the impression that I had seen a ghost.

Isaac Goldberg

The Railroad Station Which Started Charlie's Trip to America

The railroad station in Bialystok was one of the largest and most beautiful in Poland. From there, the Jews of Bialystok and their manufactured goods went all over the world. The station was a hub with connections in many directions both within the country and to other countries. The train station was also infamous, sadly, because of the slaughter of a number of Jews who were dragged out of an incoming train at the time of the 1906 pogrom in Bialystok and were murdered by station and train employees.

STEALING ACROSS THE BORDER

This happened in the time of the pogroms in Russia in 1906 when the entire Jewish community was shaken. Jewish men, women, and children were murdered at the hands of the pogromists. I decided not to remain in the "valley of death" but to travel to the free land of America where everybody had the opportunity to live in security. It was not easy for a young man to go out alone into the wide world at the age of 20; however, I realized that the future for Jews in Russia under the Czar was insecure and emigration was the only solution. I discussed this with my father and mother and they agreed with my plan.

We went to an "agent" who escorted people over the border and settled with him that for fifty rubles he would transport me across the border and guide me to Hamburg and a ship. I had no money for the journey beyond that. My parents were helpless to assist me. However, in those days my oldest brother had already gone to America, so I wrote to him asking what he could do for me so that I, too, could go to America.

But my brother could do nothing for me because he was then in the process of bringing over his own family. He therefore wrote to our uncle in California. This uncle sent me a ticket and my brother added a little money of his own, and, with good fortune, a route was opened to me.

My mother began to prepare all that I would need for my journey. She baked cookies, prepared hard little cheeses, dried salami, and she didn't forget onions, garlic, and lemons. (Lemons were one of the most important things to have with you on the ship, because when you got to sea and the ship began to toss and the nausea began to creep up from the pit of your stomach, there was no better remedy than to suck on a lemon!)

When everything was all prepared, my mother bought a little straw suitcase. All the important things were put into it, including socks, underwear, and towels. She attached a lock and handed me the key, warning me to pay close attention and not lose the key.

Then the question arose: How was I going to steal across the border carrying the suitcase? It was decided that my sister-in-law, with whom I would be traveling and who had an official permit, would take my suitcase and would send it along with her own baggage to the ship. At the ship we would meet and travel on together.

When the day comes that we are to depart, a *drozshke* (horse drawn carriage) comes up to the house. We drag out the baggage and all pile into the vehicle. The drayman strikes the little horse sharply; the horse lurches abruptly from the spot and dashes at a gallop over the cobblestones to the depot. The station is choked with people. Men and women and children with all kinds of packs are waiting for the train. A whistle is heard, a sign that the train is approaching. At that point the leave-taking begins. My mother wails and my father stands deep in worry.

"Don't forget about *Yiddishkayt!*" admonishes my father. "Don't forget to write letters," says my mother.

There is much kissing and weeping.

The train comes screeching and creaking into sight. Everybody rushes to the cars. Cries and groans can be heard as one person steps on another's feet and people push and shove; each one wants to grab a spot to sit. We find ourselves in a car as crowded as the *shul* (synagogue) on Yom Kippur at Kol Nidre time. People seem to be on top of each other.

In this condition we travel all night long. We arrive barely alive in Tshenstakhov. That is where I am to steal across the border. My sister-in-law boards another train that is to take her to the ship. I give her my little suitcase and tell to her to wait for me in Hamburg. The train departs with a whistle and I remain in the depot waiting for someone to sneak me across the border, as was agreed back home. I don't have long to wait. A Jew in a long coat comes up to me and quietly asks if I am "Khayim's passenger from Bialystok."

"Yes," I answer.

He leads me through poor streets with decaying houses. We eventually come to a large house. We go into the building, which seems almost like an inn. Inside is a large room set up with long tables. Jews are sitting around the tables and discussing the state of the world. My escort directs me to a table in the corner where other people who are going to cross the border with me are sitting. The Jew tells us to go and wash up.

A large bowl of hot potatoes is brought in as well as a bowl of borscht and a large loaf of bread. We throw ourselves upon these delicacies like hungry wolves. After we have eaten and said the blessing, the Jew shows us some bedrooms where we are to rest a bit, because we will have to try to cross the border by night.

I don't know how long I am asleep, but suddenly I feel someone awakening me. I bolt up and see the same Jew standing before me. He tells me to get ready because we will soon have to leave the inn. In a short while we depart.

He escorts us through the same crooked little streets. It is completely dark outside, the darkness of Egypt. Everything around us is silent—no sign of life. The town is sunk deeply in sleep. We go through fields and gardens until we arrive at the house of a Russian. The Jew tells us to wait there until he returns.

In a little while, the Jew comes back with a Russian guide and a wagon. He tells us to get in and warns us to be silent. He wishes us a safe crossing of the border and is soon swallowed up into the dark night.

The Russian whips the horses and we depart. My heart is heavy, and many unsettling thoughts creep into my head. Who knows if we will cross the border safely? How long we travel thus, we don't know. It seems to be forever. The Russian halts the horses, creeps around in front, and tells us to get out. He purses his lips and whistles. In the distance another whistle is heard. We stand and wait with held-in breath. A drenching rain begins. We huddle together. We are being soaked to the skin. We stand motionless and wait—for what, we have no idea. However, we notice in the darkness that a silhouette of a person begins to take shape and comes in our direction. Suddenly, we see in front of us a soldier with a rifle and a dog. We become frightened. The Russian reassures us that the soldier is one of "theirs." The soldier counts us and whispers something to the Russian. The Russian climbs back into the wagon, and we remain alone with the soldier. He tells us not to be afraid but to be quiet and do what he says and all will be well. We breathe a little easier. But the danger is far from over. The soldier signals us to follow. We creep through the mud and over rocks. The rain keeps falling. Suddenly, he tells us to stop. He listens a while in the darkness and tells us to fall down on the ground and remain still. He goes away. In a little while he returns and tells us to get up and go on. Again, we follow him. We begin to think that we will never get across to the other side as we had so fervently hoped. However, all things come to an end. In the distance little fires can be seen, a sign that we are not far from our destination. After a night of fear, soaked and muddy from head to foot, we finally reach the border.

The soldier tells us to take off our shoes. We wade through a very small stream and we are on the other side of the border. The soldier points out a house in the distance and tells us to knock on the door and we will be let in. He goes back across the border so that, Heaven forbid, no one crosses the border *illegally!* Barely alive, we drag ourselves to the house, where we are immediately let in. We look terrible. We clean ourselves up and change our clothes. Already waiting for us are hot tea and fresh rolls. After we eat, we rest awhile. We sleep for a few hours and are awakened and brought to the train. The next morning we are on the great ocean.

I will never forget the night that I stole across the border.

The ship Wandersee which Charlie sailed on to America.

MURDER BY THE DOZEN

t was on a Saturday night in winter, near Chanukah, that my
father told me this story. Outside our house a terrible blizzard
roared. It seemed as if we would be carried away, house and all.
Mama had already heated up the oven, and a delightful warmth
began to permeate the house. We children were all seated around the
stove, each of us searching for a nice, warm spot. Mama stood near
the stove preparing supper; the delicious aroma wafted in the air and
tickled our nostrils. The door suddenly opened, and papa appeared,
all covered with snow.

"A pleasant week to all of you," he said.

"A pleasant week and a pleasant year," we all responded.

"It's truly deathly cold outside, but here in the house it's like
Paradise. You have no idea what is going on out there."

Mama went over to Papa and said, "Go to the porch and shake
the snow off."

"Never mind the snow," Papa replied. "What about supper?"
"Everything will be ready in about half an hour, and then we'll eat."
Papa looked at us and smiled. "If it has to take another half hour, I'll
go out and shake off the snow and then will tell you all a story that
happened not far from our city of Bialystok."

In a few moments he returned, and began his tale.

"You know about a district called Stakhisheltzia. In that district there lived an innkeeper named Tzitrin. The Tzitrin family were the Count's tenants for many generations. Just as the district went from one Count to another by inheritance, so did the tenants pass down from generation to generation. The last tenant of whom I will tell you was a very pious and scholarly Jew. When still a young man, he was ordained by very great rabbis. However, he didn't want to earn his living as a rabbi because he didn't want to use his learning for mercenary purposes. When his father died, he took over the business just as his father and grandfather before him had done. Although he was very occupied with his business, he did not neglect the Torah.

The years sped by; he had children, married them off, and lived to see grandchildren.

Tzitrin took great pleasure in providing hospitality to people. In fact, he had a reputation as an excellent host. Whoever opened his door could be assured of a cordial welcome. He regularly had a *minyan* (ten men who assemble for prayer) in his house. The poverty-stricken residents of the district would come to him on Shabbos for communal prayers.

When he reached his older years, he gathered his children together and said to them, "Dear children, I am old; I want you to take over the business. From today on I want to devote myself entirely to the Torah." From that day onward, he studied Torah day and night.

One day, early in the morning, just before Tisha B'Av (a time of mourning the destruction of the Jerusalem Temple), a visitor appeared with a pack on his back.

"I've come a long way," he said, "and I'm very tired. I'm going to Bialystok, but since it's just before Tisha B'Av, I would like to stay here to say *Kines*" (a prayer of lamentation.)

Needless to say, the visitor spent the day. In the evening, neighboring Jews came together to say *Ma'ariv* (the evening prayer) and *Kines*. After prayers, the men sat together and talked of many things. Afterwards, late in the evening, the men dispersed to their homes. The visitor was shown where to sleep and went to bed. The old man remained awake, still studying.

Early the next morning, when the first neighbor came to the door, it seemed to him that the house was too silent. He became uneasy and opened the door. He saw a horrific scene before him: On the floor near the door, old Tzitrin was lying in a pool of blood. The neighbor raised an alarm and the people from the town ran quickly and gathered at the house. A deathly apprehension enveloped everyone. When they went into the other rooms, they found a body in every one of them. The place looked like a slaughterhouse. The family consisted of twelve people, and all twelve were dead. The murderers didn't even spare the young children.

The authorities in Bialystok were immediately notified. The police arrived with a magistrate to investigate the crime. They interrogated the neighbors but couldn't find any trace of the murderer. The whole city of Bialystok was appalled by the terrible murders.

The magistrate decided to call all the neighbors together and said to them, "Does anyone remember seeing a stranger in the vicinity at the time of the murders?"

One of the neighbors remembered about the visitor in the Tzitrin home on the night of the murders. He was not found among the victims. The authorities immediately raised the alarm to search for the "visitor."

Hundreds of people from all around came to the funeral of the twelve victims. The wails rose up to the heart of Heaven. They were all buried in a single grave, and a large memorial was placed over their resting place. When Rosh HaShanah arrived, or Tisha B'Av, when people would go to the cemetery to visit their parents' graves, mourners would also stop and weep at the grave of these victims.

The search for the "visitor" went on at a feverish tempo. They searched for him everywhere... in hospices for the poor, in poorhouses, in synagogues. But no one found a trace of him.

Three months after the murders, in a small town not far from Bialystok, a stranger appeared in one of the synagogues. He sat in a corner near the stove and prayed the Psalms. One of the congregants noticed him and informed the police. He was arrested and interrogated. Where was he from? Where was he at the time of the murders? He finally broke down and confessed the horrible murders. He said he was the leader of a band of robbers.

"In my youth I was a horse thief," he said. "And when the police of the whole region knew me quite well, I decided to give up my 'profession' of stealing horses. I gathered together several others like myself and we decided to rob and kill. To that purpose I grew a beard and wore a *kapoteh* (caftan). I went from district to district, from town to town asking for a night's lodging. When everyone was asleep, I spied out what was of value in the house. We would then rob the house in the dark of night. If we managed to get away unnoticed, we didn't harm anyone, but if anyone woke up, we would kill him. In the Tzitrin house, a child woke up and began to cry, so we immediately suffocated it. Meanwhile, the child's father woke up, so we killed him, too. In order to cover up these killings, we murdered the entire family."

The murderer was sentenced to death. In those days, a murderer was "quartered." (This means that each limb was severed separately.) They executed him in the middle of the marketplace in Bialystok. I am told that this story can be found in a book of records in Bialystok so that these victims could be remembered forever.

Shops in the center of Bialystok pre-World War I.

A SERPENT'S TOOTH

Many years ago, a certain bookseller's shop could be found on one of the main streets in Bialystok. The man was called "the Kalner," because he came from a small town called "Kalne." He was a pious Jew, very clever, and very learned in Torah... a man of the "old school." He had an eastern seat (a prestigious place) in the big synagogue and was respected by everyone with whom he came into contact.

This bookseller had an only daughter, twenty years of age, who was a great beauty, and who had graduated from the gymnasium. Life for the parents and the daughter was quiet and happy. The Kalner made a good living and the parents were grateful and thanked God for their bright and beautiful daughter. And, of course, they hoped to derive great joy from her.

However, a great tragedy suddenly befell the parents. And this is how it happened.

A new *garodovoy* (policeman) was assigned to the neighborhood where the family had the bookshop. He was a tall and handsome Russian. Soon, the young girl and the handsome young man began to fall in love.

For a long time no one knew about it; however, since Heaven and Earth vowed that there is no such thing as a secret, people began to notice that something was going on between the girl and the

Russian. Eventually the parents heard about the situation. When they found out, it was like thunder out of a clear sky. They questioned their daughter, but she denied everything. "Enemies are making up stories about me," she insisted.

The parents began to keep a closer eye on her. Then, one evening, they found her in a dark corner kissing the young man. There could now be no doubt that something was going on between them.

Both father and mother pleaded with the girl not to bring shame upon them; they wept, they threatened to kill themselves. It seemed that the parents' entreaties had actually influenced her, when suddenly she disappeared. It was discovered that she had gone to church and planned to convert.

The house soon reverberated with the parents' anguished laments, with their weeping and wailing.

In desperation, they ran to the priest, fell on their knees before him, and pleaded with him to give them back their daughter. The priest replied that he could not help them because she came of her own free will. However, he did grant them permission to see her.

When the daughter was told that her parents wanted to see her, she refused to see them. They returned home, heartbroken. People tried to comfort the parents by telling them that this was the will of Heaven, but they could not be comforted.

A few weeks later the church bells rang. A large number of Gentiles gathered, and with great pageantry led the girl to the church for her conversion. The parents mourned her as if she had died, and the Jews of the city wished that all her future endeavors be unsuccessful.

But this was not the end of the story. Out of spite, she set

up her home very near her parents and set about to hurt and
humiliate them however she could. For example, she used to wait
until the Jews were on their way to synagogue on Saturday morning
and would then bring out the basin of slops and feed the pigs so the
Jews could see her. Whenever a Jew passed her house, she would
curse and insult him.

However, the Lord of the Universe does not overlook sin.
Little by little, her misfortune began. Her husband would get drunk
and beat her. (She would often be seen on the street with blackened
eyes.) He would nag her to go to her parents to demand her dowry;
and when that didn't help, he would get even more drunk and go to
the father's shop himself and bang on the table demanding the dowry.

Because he was a *garodovoy,* the young man made a great
deal of trouble for the family. From day to day the parents grew
more depressed. They weren't seen in the street, they didn't go to
synagogue, and when it became too much for the soul to bear, they
gave up their business and left Bialystok.

The convert remained in town and flaunted her conversion.
One Saturday, as usual, she carried out the basin of slops for the pigs.
Suddenly, she fell, and because she was far along in her pregnancy,
went into labor. She gave birth to a stillborn baby, became very ill
and suffered many days until she died.

Everyone saw that the punishment of Heaven had befallen her.

Jewish shops in Białystok with German, Yiddish, and Polish signs, during the German occupation of the city during World War I. (Left to right) M. Chodorowsky's Wholesale Smoked Meats; Yitskhok Baran, Shoemaker; Wine, Beer, and Tea. (Tomasz Wisniewski)

A SOLDIER'S TALE

y friend began to tell his story. "I was a 'Daddy's boy.' I never pictured that I would have to go into military service, but the recruiter had other ideas. No matter what price my father was willing to pay so that I would not be drafted, nothing helped. I became a soldier, and I was sent to Saratover Gubernya.

When I arrived in my regiment I was assigned to the fourth company. Only four Jews were in my company; I immediately became acquainted with these Jewish soldiers and asked how things were going for them in the service. They replied that it wouldn't be bad except that a short while earlier a company commander had arrived who was a rotten person. He tormented the soldiers nearly to death. The soldiers hated him like death itself. Whatever he could devise to humiliate the soldiers he did with sadistic pleasure. In the short time he had come to the company it had become a veritable Gehenna. He would beat a soldier nearly to death for the slightest infraction. However, he was very pleased with any soldier who knew the *slozshve* (the military manual). Therefore they advised me that I should begin to study the manual as soon as possible so my service would be easier. I knew Russian, so I attacked the manual and in a few weeks I knew the whole volume by heart.

The time came when the commander was to come to the

company to examine the new recruits. They ran around as if without heads. They were country bumpkins, blockheads, and simply couldn't pick their way through the three-deep titles of the Czar and his family.

The commander arrived. The company was lined up in formation. The officer went from one to another asking questions. The peasants didn't know their hands from their feet. Slaps flew right and left. Rage inflamed him. He approached me and looked straight into my face. "A Jew?"

"Exactly so, your honor."

He then begins to toss questions at me. I answer precisely plus provide a commentary on each question. He attempts to confuse me but it doesn't work. I see that his expression is softening.

"You *moozshikes!*" he shouts at the soldiers. "Here is a Jew barely a short time in the barracks and he knows everything like a veteran, you blockheads!"

He calls me out of the rank, gives me a slap on the back, and announces, "Young man, you're going to get an extra ration of bread and a day's leave to go into town. And I want you to take these *moozshikes* in hand and pound a little *slozshve* into their thick heads." I set to work with those peasants and practiced with them every day until they began to grasp the manual.

When the commander came again two weeks later and listened to the soldiers, he couldn't believe that they had learned so much in so little time.

From that time on things in the company were very good for me. I received various privileges, and the soldiers would have gone through fire and water for me.

During my second year of service, a Jewish recruit from Poland arrived, a fine fellow. However, he got it into his head that he wasn't going to do his military service. I tried to make him understand that he had to make peace with the idea that he was a soldier and to knock out of his head that he wasn't going to be one. I used to tell him, "Attend to the *slozshve*. I will study with you and things will go better for you."

However, he paid no attention to me and stubbornly insisted that he would not be a soldier. His life in the barracks was a Gehenna. He had to do every dirty job. He spent more time in the guardhouse than with the company.

The same commander was still with us. One day the idea came into his head to check on the soldiers who were standing guard duty to see if they were observing the rules of the week. About a half-mile from the barracks was a munitions depot tucked away in the woods... a very isolated place. He decided that he would go there at night to see what the sentry was doing... to make sure he wasn't asleep. To be asleep at one's post merited severe punishment. The instructions were that when a soldier at his post noticed something, he had to call out "Halt" three times. If he received no reply, he was permitted to shoot, no matter what.

It so happened that it befell the Polish Jew to be at the sentry post on a dark, end-of-the-month night. Everything was enveloped in darkness. It was said in the company that some soldiers on guard duty had noticed something among the trees like the shape of a person. Some believed these reports, others said it was just imagination. It was with this idea in his head that our Polish Jew set about guarding the munitions depot. About halfway through the night he thought he saw something moving among the trees. He strained his eyes in the darkness.

"Halt!" he shouted and raised his gun. No answer, but the silhouette came closer.

"Halt!" he shouted a second time. Again no answer, only his own echo.

"Halt!" he shouted a third time, and since he heard no answer the third time, he shot straight into the silhouette.

Hearing the shot, the soldiers who were scheduled to relieve him that week came running with their senior officer to find out what happened. He told them that he noticed something among the trees and that he shouted "Halt" three times and when he received no answer he shot at the silhouette. They all ran immediately to see what happened and discovered that the person who had been shot was their commander. He was dead.

They brought him back to the barracks and there was a terrible commotion. Our soldier was arrested. In his defense he said that he felt keenly the responsibilities of a sentry. However, he hadn't realized that it was the commander.

He was freed.

The soldiers silently blessed him for getting rid of the commander.

TWO FRIENDS

As a young boy in *kheder* (Hebrew school) I became friends with a fellow about the same age as I who was called Shloyme. From the first day we met we immediately became very close friends. We both came from poor homes and had much in common. In school, we shared the food our mothers gave us and often visited each other's homes. The folks in town talked about us as if we were David and Jonathan. Time doesn't stand still, however, and we grew up. We both joined a Zionist organization and our friendship remained solid.

There was one thing, however, in which Shloyme was better than I. He had a beautiful voice and sang in the synagogue. The cantor held him in great esteem. I got great pleasure out of hearing Shloyme sing.

One day Shloyme came to me and said that his family was going to America. For me, this was terrible news. I couldn't imagine how I could live without Shloyme's friendship, but the family went away and I was left alone. I missed my friend very much, but eventually got used to the idea that I had to make new friends. But I never forgot Shloyme.

At first, he would write to me often. Then, little by little, the letters grew fewer until he stopped writing entirely. Then came the terrible days of the pogroms, and I, too, decided to go to America.

When I came to the "Golden Land", I, like all the "greeners," endured all the trials of Gehenna.

In time, my situation improved. I got married and worked hard to earn a living. However, I never stopped looking for Shloyme.

After a few years in New York, I realized that I couldn't accomplish anything there so I decided to move to "the country." I chose Connecticut, settled in a small town and in time became a resident, a member of the synagogue, got involved in community affairs and was glad that I had left New York.

One Shabbos before the "Days of Awe" there was talk that a cantor was being brought in for the holidays. The cantor came on a trial basis, pleased the congregation, and they arranged with him to be our community leader. That Shabbos I was not at home and when I returned I was told that the cantor was a *yakar hamtziot* (precious find).

The Days of Awe approached. When *slikhes* (prayers said before the High Holidays) was to be said, the synagogue was packed. The cantor appeared. I saw that a middle-aged man entered, a *hederet panim* (beautiful physically and spiritually). He approached the lectern. The *shamash* (sexton) rapped on the *bimeh* (pulpit). The synagogue became quiet. The cantor begins to sing "Kaddish." His voice is very pleasing. The words slip easily from his mouth. It seems to me that this cantor is somehow familiar. I could have sworn that I saw or heard him someplace. The thought won't let me rest. I look at the congregation. Everyone is enthralled with his singing. After the service, everyone runs up to him to congratulate him. I, too, go up to him and say "Shalom" and congratulations. I look straight into his eyes. He notices my curiosity and asks:

"Tell me, friend, why are you looking at me so intently?"

"I want to tell you, cantor, you seem very familiar to me. Tell me, what's your name?"

"My name," he says, "is Shloyme."

"From what town in Europe did you come?"

He smiles, and says to me, "If you're interested, I come from Bialystok."

When I heard where he came from, I couldn't contain myself any longer.

"Shloyme, my friend, don't you recognize me? I'm Zakharia, your childhood friend."

When he heard my name, he became confused for a moment and looked at me keenly. Then he embraced me heartily. We hugged each other.

The people around us watched the scene and gaped at us.

It's unnecessary to say that I brought Shloyme home with me. He stayed with me during the High Holy Days. We told each other what we had endured during all the years we hadn't seen each other. After that time, we were again David and Jonathan.

A Jewish tailor in Poland, c 1910.

THE GENERAL

n our city there lived a tailor who used to travel around the
various districts sewing fur pelts for the Russians in exchange
for a little flour, a few eggs, some groats, and other similar
foodstuffs. In this way he supported his family, which consisted
of a wife and five children... four girls and a boy. Needless to say,
they were very poor, yet the tailor was content, thanked God for
his blessings, and accepted without protest his poverty-stricken
life. The family lived a quiet and modest life until the Russians
passed that infamous decree that drafted small boys into the army.
The poor tailor's family was not spared. One can only imagine
how terrible it was when he returned from his travels one day and
discovered that his only son had been taken away to the army. Both
mother and father ran about as if they were demented, literally
banging their heads against the walls, becoming deathly ill from
anguish. Nothing could console them.

Time, however, has great healing power. Eventually the tailor
resumed his trade and again traveled around the various districts
sewing fur pelts for the Russians. Nothing further was heard about
the boy.

Years come and years go, and the time came when the tailor
could no longer travel to practice his trade. His wife had died, and
one of his daughters brought him to live with her. He spent his

days praying; the pages of the old prayer book had become soaked through with the tears he had shed over his lost son.

Eventually, the time came for one of his grandsons to be drafted into the Czar's army. He was sent to one of the very distant Russian provinces and endured all that a new recruit must bear. In his second year of service, he was transferred to a musician's unit. Because he was a musician, his life became more bearable. He no longer had to participate in maneuvers, but only had to play for parades and for the parties of the "bigwigs."

One day the musician was notified that an important official was coming, and a great ball was being given in his honor. On the day that the ball was to take place, the orchestra dressed up as if for a holiday and played for the assembled guests, who ate and drank lavishly. Although the wine gushed like water, the musician noticed that the general with the golden epaulets... the honored guest... was drinking very little, and seemed to be watching him all evening. The musician wondered what it meant. Could it be that his playing pleased the general more than that of the other musicians? And something else wasn't clear to him... somehow this officer was different from the other officials. While the others were all dead drunk, he was sitting as if he were unaware of the revelry around him.

From time to time he seemed to be looking off in the distance, as if trying to remember something.

The party ended. The Jewish musician went back to his barracks and lay down on his bed, but could not fall asleep.

The next morning he was called into the administrative office and was told that the general had sent his servant for him; it was necessary to go see the general. When he heard this, he became frightened, but then calmed down because he realized that he had done nothing disrespectful toward the general. He went with the servant to the general's quarters. The general told him to come in.

He entered and remained standing near the fireplace. The general turned toward him.

"Come closer and sit down here, near me," he said.

With shaking steps the musician went over to the indicated place and sat down. The general looked at him carefully and then spoke to him softly.

"Don't be afraid of me. Just answer a few questions. Tell me, are you from the town of Pravaslav?"

"No, honored sir," he replied. "I am a Jew."

"What town are you from?"

The musician mentioned the name of the town and also gave his own name.

The general was quiet for a moment, apparently deep in thought, his head bowed between his hands. When he looked up, the musician saw that his eyes were full of tears.

"Tell me," said the general, "are your grandparents still alive?"

"My grandfather is still alive and is very old. He is now living with my mother. My grandmother has been dead for a long time. Until the last day of her life she mourned her child, who was taken by force from her. But please tell me why, honored sir, do you ask all these questions? Why does my family interest you?"

After a brief silence, the general turned toward the musician.

"I am going to entrust you with a very great secret. No one

must ever hear about it. I am your uncle. I am that nine-year-old boy who was torn away from his parents and made into a soldier. Your name and the name of the town from which you came have convinced me of this."

The musician sat as if turned to stone. "The general is my uncle?" he thought. "How can that be? This must all be a dream."

But the general immediately got up from his seat, approached the musician, and began to kiss him and weep. When he had calmed down a bit, he told the musician what had happened from the beginning: how he had been distanced from his parents and the pain and woes he had endured while indentured to a peasant in the village to which he had been assigned until he would reach the age of 21 and go into the army. "Hunger, beatings, and hard labor from early in the morning until late at night... this is what my dreadful life was. I was constantly being tormented and exhorted to convert. I endured all the agonies and didn't want to agree. And when I finally arrived at my army unit, a new wave of torment and harassment began... beatings and insults. How many times I wanted to take my own life!"

"I was a good soldier," he continued, "and I was urged to convert to further my career. They described a wonderful future if I accepted the Russian Orthodox faith. I didn't resist, and I converted. I was immediately sent to officers' school and rose from rank to rank to where I am now. I have a wife and children, I'm rich, but not happy. I've been thinking lately about returning to the Jewish religion. My meeting you strengthened my desire to go through with this plan. I have decided to leave my wife and children and go to a large city near my former home. I will convert back to Judaism, and no one will know about my situation. I will pretend to be a merchant who returns to business... naturally, under a different name. I will go to the town where my family lives under the guise of a person who just recently discovered his relatives. I will confide in my father about who I am. I think I will be able to succeed in carrying this through."

The two men parted. The musician went back to his regiment but was unable to get this event out of his mind. Three months later, he received a letter from his uncle that everything went according to plan. He was now a Jew again and happy that he went through with his decision.

View of a street with wooden houses in prewar Bialystok.

A COMMOTION IN THE HORSE STALL

What I am about to relate to the readers of the "Amerikaner" happened to me thirty-five years ago. At that time I lived in a small town in Connecticut. It was in the middle of winter. Dreadful snow and cold were continuous. A few friends and I were sitting around a warm stove and chatting about the hard winter that had been going on so long that it wasn't even worthwhile to leave one's house to earn a few dollars. From time to time we glanced out through the frosty window at the blizzard that refused to calm down.

Suddenly we heard someone at the door; my brother appeared, covered with snow from head to foot.

"Oh, it's so lovely and warm here," he said. "But I didn't come here to get warm. I was just notified that the wife of 'B,' the farmer, died and you will need to come with me to maintain a vigil during the night because 'B' is alone in the house. His children are all in New York and they will not be able to get here until morning; no train will be coming into town today."

To tell the truth, I didn't have any great desire to leave the warm stove and spend a night with a dead body. However, *bekavod ha met* (respect for the dead) is not a small thing. I didn't want to decline, so I put on my winter fur coat and my fur-lined shoes and set off with my brother to the farm, which was about a mile from town. As yet there were no automobiles in town because in those days nobody earned enough money to be able to buy an automobile. Traveling with horse and wagon was not an option because the roads were piled high with snow, and we would surely have gotten stuck on the way. We had no other choice but to set off on foot.

The way was difficult—the freezing air burned, the snow beat against our faces. It took us a long time until we came to the farm. Half frozen, we fell into the house, warmed ourselves a bit, and did what we had to do for the deceased. Recovering a bit, we noted the poverty of the house; there was hardly a chair to sit on. We threw a few pieces of wood in the stove, and each took our Book of Psalms from our pockets and began to pray.

It became dark. The little flames from the burning candles cast lonely shadows on the walls. Everything around was silent except for the storm that tore at the roof. It seemed as if ghosts were dancing on the roof.

The hours stretched out as if they were made of pitch. Uneasiness enveloped me.

We recited the Psalms and attempted to drive away the lonely thoughts. Little by little, those who were with me began to doze; to keep from falling asleep, I began to pray with added enthusiasm and fervor.

About the middle of the night my companions were sound asleep. The farmer, exhausted from having cared so long for his sick wife, and my brother, a hard worker, could not resist the temptation to snatch a few winks near the warm stove. I began to think of a verse: *Ma yitron la-adam b'khol amalo (Is it worth the effort?)*

Suddenly, I seem to hear a commotion in the horse stall. I remember that when I was a young boy in *kheder*, the rebbe would tell us stories about ghosts... how they gather together at night in horse stalls and ride the animals furiously; if one comes to the stall at first light one finds the horses exhausted, completely covered with foam and barely able to stand on their feet.

Knowing this farmer's mare, I am sure that she can't kick with very much force because she is a real "Mendele's mare." I try to drive away the foolish thoughts about ghosts, but the commotion continues.

I awaken my companions and ask them if they hear any noise. Half asleep, they reply that they hear nothing, and they go back to sleep. But... dear God... I do hear a commotion. I'm wide awake; I can't sleep. Why don't the others hear what I hear? I become uneasy so I wake up my brother and tell him that we need to investigate loud noises in the stall.

We leave the farmer in the house and my brother and I light a lantern and go forth. As we enter the stall, the mare greets us with a whinny, apparently happy that we came to visit, and starts to chew on some hay. We look around, but find no evidence of anything out of order. The mare is not covered with foam, as my rebbe once described. I begin to wonder what's happening with me. I really did hear banging and kicking, as if hundreds of ghosts were running around.

We go back into the house. My brother and the farmer go back to sleep. I return to my prayers, and again I hear the same racket. The hours drag by so slowly that it seems as though it will never again be morning. I sit thus at my prayers until the first rays of daylight. When it's fully light, I awaken my brother and we leave the farm.

When I returned to town and told people what had happened during the night, everyone laughed at me.

In spite of the fact that I know that seeing or hearing "ghosts" is the product of one's imagination, until this day I don't understand how, fully awake, I heard a commotion in the horse stall that no one else heard.

THE INSPECTOR

n the days of the last Tzar Nicholas, the lives of Jews in the Pale of Settlement were very difficult. Many occupations were not permitted them, so their lives were very stifled. They managed to cope somehow; they patched clothes, repaired shoes, and one way or another were able to survive in their poverty. There were, of course, a few rich men in the district, but by far the majority were paupers.

The people who suffered the most, however, were the shopkeepers and those who had small stalls in the marketplace. What little livelihood there was had to be earned in spite of the inspectors who used to appear from time to time in the marketplace to torment the poor shopkeepers. Jews had no right to have a license to sell things, so they had to work around this problem somehow. What they did was to bribe the local police commissioner so that they would be warned when an inspector was coming. As soon as they were told, they emptied all their shelves, and when the inspector appeared, he found empty shops. Not only that, but he also received a bribe so he could conveniently "forget" his inspection. This type of thing was bearable when the inspector was a "taker," but if he refused a bribe, the situation got really serious for the shopkeepers.

To their dismay, there came a time when an inspector was

assigned to the town who was said not only to refuse bribes, but also to be violently anti-Semitic. This man, a convert from Judaism, spoke excellent Yiddish.

This was the beginning of bitter times for the poor shopkeepers. The local supervisor was approached and was offered money to have the inspector transferred someplace else, but nothing came of it. Realizing that they couldn't survive with him around, the shopkeepers got together and decided to get rid of him another way: some young men were found who undertook to give him a taste of his own medicine.

One night, when the inspector was on his way home, he was grabbed, a sack was thrown over his head, he was tossed into a wagon, and was driven to the river for "ritual purification." When the wagon stopped and he heard the sound of the water, he understood what they planned to do with him. He began to plead for his life. He would repent, he said, and would go far away if they would only free him. The young men told him, "We will let you go this time, but if you don't keep your word, we won't be so forgiving next time."

He was tossed back into the wagon and left alongside the road close to town. He managed to get out of the sack and went home.

Early the next morning he showed up in the marketplace with the police, trying to identify the men who had taken him to the river. But it was like looking for a needle in a haystack. And since he couldn't positively identify those who had participated, no one was arrested.

Now, he promised, he would really make the Jews' lives miserable. And he kept his word. However spiteful he had been in the past, he now became a thousand times worse. He was constantly in a murderous rage. The shopkeepers were terrified. Some people now regretted that they had trusted his word and let him go.

Then, the inspector didn't appear in the marketplace for a day or two. The people began to breathe a little easier, thinking that he had been transferred somewhere else. They thanked God that they had gotten rid of the anti-Semite.

Sometime later, before Passover, when the ice melted, the river washed up a body. There was a great tumult in town; the police arrived, but the body was in such bad condition that it was not possible to identify him. A high official arrived, along with some investigators, but their efforts were futile. They were unable to connect anyone to the dead man. After a long investigation, they had to go back with empty hands.

No one in town doubted that the body was that of the inspector, but no one was ever punished.

The Old Synagogue in Bialystok.

GETTING EVEN WITH THE RABBI

T he sort of *kheder (Hebrew school)* we had in old-time Russia is well known to all. And as bad as the conditions were in the *kheders,* the *talmud torahs* were even worse. Like every community institution, the *talmud torahs* (primary schools for boys) were entrusted to supervisors and trustees, but those responsible in the community paid little attention to the poor children.

My father was not a rich man and was not able to enroll me in *kheder* until I was ready to study in the *talmud torah.* The rabbi with whom I came to study was one of the old-time *melamids* (teachers) who believed that to make devout Jews of his students required being harsh and being generous with physical punishment. My rabbi held firmly to this idea and we children were not to be envied. All day long he walked around the *kheder* with a whip in his hand. For the slightest thing he beat the children without mercy.

The rabbi was a small man, thin, and always angry. One never saw a pleasant look on his face. He came from a small town not far from Bialystok and rarely saw his family, only returning home for Passover and Sukkos. He was very miserly, hardly allowing himself to buy a bit of bread. He lived on what each student had to bring him from home. One would bring a piece of bread, another a few potatoes, others some groats, a few pieces of sugar, an onion, a bit of garlic, and sometimes a few vegetables. This is what he survived on;

this is how he lived from one time to the next. He slept in the *kheder* on a hard bench. It was no wonder that he was always bitter and took out his bitterness on us children.

We *kheder* students hated him with a passion and thought about ways to avenge ourselves. The opportunity arrived just before the first night of Chanukah. The rabbi didn't have to spend even a few *groshen* on Chanukah candles because he owned a Chanukah lamp that burned oil. He took out the lamp, poured in some oil, made a wick from a bit of cotton that he tore from his winter coat, and prepared the lamp for the coming *mitzvah (ritual obligation.)* It's true that the lamp didn't emit much light, but the rabbi was pleased that he didn't have to spend any money for candles.

Watching the rabbi puttering around the Chanukah lamp, we youngsters got the idea that this was the time to take our revenge. We talked among ourselves and decided that when the rabbi went to say the *maariv* prayer we would spill out the oil and replace it with water. Of course, the wicks wouldn't ignite. We swore on our *tzitzit* (tassels on undergarments worn by Orthodox Jews) that no matter what happened later, we would all be united and would not admit who had thought up the plan.

Just as soon as the rabbi went to say the *maariv* prayer, we went to work, spilled out the oil from the lamp, poured in water, and returned the lamp to where it had been so that he would not be suspicious. Hearing the rabbi return, we bent our heads over our *Gemaras* and pretended to be diligently studying as if nothing had happened.

When the rabbi entered he told us to stop studying; he put on his Sabbath coat with its sash, said a special Chanukah prayer, lit the *shamas* (helper) candle, said the candle-lighting prayer for Chanukah, said the shehekhaynu prayer, and held the *shamas* to the wicks, but none would ignite. The wicks sputtered but refused to catch fire. The rabbi gets angry, yelling

"Nu... ha... nu... ha" but he won't stop trying, hoping that maybe they will catch fire, but to no avail. He can't understand what's happening. He picks up the lid of the lamp and looks in. He becomes incredibly angry. He peers right through us with his glowering look and shouts, "Bastards! A curse on your idleness. I'll skin you alive! I'll call Shimon the Mashgiakh!" (kosher supervisor)

When we heard the name of Shimon the Mashgiakh we became terrified. Shimon is a brute. To fall into his hands meant one should first say *vidui,* (a confession of sins before death). It didn't take long and Shimon appeared with his strap. He began to beat our poor, skinny bodies, yelling, "Bastards, I'll beat you to death!" We were silent; no one said a word. We bear the blows without protest and keep quiet.

Shimon saw that he could not get a word out of us so he stopped beating us and said that the next day he would come with the *gabai* (trustee) who would open our mouths for us. Meanwhile, the rabbi silently poured out the water from the Chanukah lamp, once again filled it with oil, blessed the Chanukah lights, said the Chanukah *hallu* prayer, and told us to go home.

It's true that we were severely beaten, but it was worthwhile. We got even with the rabbi.

Białystok. A street in the Chanajki neighborhood.

A POOR BOY IS NOT DESTINED FOR JOY

The city in which I was born was hardly different from all the other cities in the Pale of Settlement. We had some rich men, but the vast majority were paupers who struggled to make a living for their families. My father was such a poor man.

Ordinary childish pleasures were unknown to me. When I went to *kheder* (Hebrew school) I was fiercely jealous of the rich boys who brought fresh rolls and butter to school, and sometimes even a pear or an apple for dessert. On winter nights when the *rebbe* let us go home, the rich boys would rush from the *kheder* with their lighted lanterns throwing golden rays on the white snow and singing *Shuvi, shuvi, ha Shulamit* (from "Song of Songs"). I felt as if the very life were going out of me. Finally, I asked my father to buy me a lantern so that I, too, could carry it in the dark and sing *Shuvi, shuvi, ha Shulamit* like the other boys. My father told me that a real lantern cost a *gilden*, and he couldn't afford it. But he comforted me. "I'll make you a paper lantern that will be much prettier than the metal ones the other boys have."

No sooner said than done. My father set to work and made me a lantern of pleated paper that was beautiful to look at. He smeared it with oil so that the light would show through better. I went off to *kheder* with my lantern. All that day nothing that I studied stayed in my head. I waited impatiently for it to get dark so that I could go outside with my lantern and be like the other boys. Night came. The *rebbe* sent us home, and like always, the children rushed outside, swinging their lanterns and singing *Shuvi, shuvi ha Shulamit,* and this time, so did I. There was no limit to my joy. However, my happiness did not last long. Suddenly, my lantern caught fire and in a minute nothing was left of it but a bit of ash. I cried bitterly because of this great tragedy that had befallen me. It seemed as though a poor boy like me was not destined to have a bit of joy.

Meanwhile, time hurried by. When I was eleven years old my mother had me apprenticed to a furniture maker. I had to labor three years without pay; if I stayed the three years I would receive twenty rubles. The work was hard, but I worked willingly because I knew that I was a poor boy and this was my destiny.

Just as I had once yearned to have a lantern, now I wanted a pair of galoshes. New galoshes were out of the question, but in the marketplace was a Jew who bought old galoshes and repaired them. He would patch the holes with a special liquid that he ordered by mail from Warsaw. Nobody knew the secret of this special liquid; he would do his repairs at night in a secluded place. Purchasing such a pair of galoshes was possible with a few *gilden*—but how could I get the few *gilden* I needed?

I decided not to spend the few *kopecks* that I would get from time to time when we would deliver a sofa or a bed to a bride and groom. Several months passed. I counted my fortune and saw that I had enough money to buy the galoshes. I went to the marketplace and looked over the Jew's wares. After much bargaining we came to terms on a price of 65 *kopecks*. I took the galoshes and ran joyfully home; my happiness was unbounded. But my dream didn't last long. When I looked carefully at the galoshes, I decided that they weren't shiny enough. Undismayed, I went out, bought some lacquer, and applied it to the galoshes; they looked like new. (Who could have known the consequences?) When the lacquer dried, I tried to pull the galoshes on over my shoes, but it was a disaster. The galoshes shattered; apparently the lacquer had dried them out so much that they crumbled like an egg *kikhel* (type of brittle cookie). The galoshes turned out to be a disaster just like the lantern.

It seems that a poor boy is just not destined to have a little joy.

MYSTERY IN A SMALL TOWN

Not far from town lived a farmer in his sixties whom we'll call "Max." In those days it was the custom for foreigners to work a while in America, save a few dollars, and then return to Europe. A Pole came to work for Max; he, like many others, thought to save some money and return to Poland, buy a bit of land and be together with his family again. However, when the Pole asked the farmer to be paid for his work, the farmer always convinced him that if he were paid, he would drink up his earnings and never have enough to return home.

"If you want a drink," Max would say, "here's a few dollars, go get drunk, and what I owe you I'll keep for you until you're ready to return home."

Time went by and after the Pole had been working for Max for a few years he started thinking about returning home, buying some property, and becoming his own boss.

Then, the neighbors noticed that no one had seen Max's worker for a while. When Max was asked about it, he said that one Sunday the worker went into town and never returned. Since the man had been thinking about returning home for a while, it was likely that he left without so much as a "goodbye." But Max's believability about the worker who disappeared was questioned.

Someone went to the police and detectives came. They looked and searched but found no sign of the missing Pole.

In that area in those days a young Jew peddled goods to the farmers. He would also show up from time to time in the town; everyone knew him. Two days before Passover the peddler appeared in town and entered one of the stores. He chatted with the storekeeper who asked him if he had somewhere to spend Passover. "If not," said the storekeeper, "come be my guest for the holiday." The peddler thanked him for the invitation but said that he had already arranged to spend Passover at Max's house. The peddler parted ways with the storekeeper, threw his pack on his back, and left the store.

Six months passed and the peddler didn't return to town. That was not his usual custom, and since the story with the Pole was still fresh in everyone's memory, people began to wonder if there was a connection between the Pole and the peddler. In a short period of time two men had disappeared and there was no sign of them.

In the meantime, the police were still pursuing the investigation, although they hadn't made much progress. One of the detectives refused to give up. He asked to be relieved of his regular duties and to be given a period of time to devote himself entirely to this case. He was granted this request.

One day a man arrived at Max's farm dressed in workman's clothes and asked for a job. Max hired him. The detective, in his disguise as the simple laborer, worked efficiently, milking the cows, working in the fields, and chopping wood. Max was very satisfied with his new hired hand; however, whenever the detective was left alone, he began to search and hunt through the area. He examined every little tree, every patch of grass, but the weeks ran by and he found no trace of the missing men.

One day when he was alone, he went into the nearby woods, stamping his feet and searching among the fallen leaves. Suddenly, he stepped on some soft earth. Quickly he began to dig and found something wrapped in a sack. He unwrapped the sack and found a decayed corpse. The detective immediately phoned the police.

The order was given to arrest Max. When Max heard what was found, he ran to his friend's house, crying: "Save me, I'm an innocent victim. Somebody buried the body on my farm but I did not commit the murder. Help me escape to New York City; I'll stay there a while because I'm sure that the real murderer will be found."

The friend gave him the address of his daughter and Max went into hiding. When the police went to his house, he was gone.

When Max got to New York, the first thing he did was shave off his beard. He then found work under a false name. No matter how hard the police sought him, they were unsuccessful. Max disappeared as if swallowed up by the sea.

The police offered a thousand dollar reward to whoever revealed his whereabouts. And it was his friend who turned him in. Max was arrested and brought back to town.

What went on then in town cannot be described. Max wept and complained that he was innocent. When he was asked why he ran away to New York, he answered that he did it because he was sure that the police would continue to search and would find the real murderer.

The trial lasted several weeks. Max kept shouting that he was innocent. His defense lawyers did the best they could under the circumstances, but when the jury went out to deliberate, they quickly brought in their verdict: guilty of first degree murder. His sentence was appealed to a higher court, but was upheld. Even the governor didn't want to get involved in changing the verdict.

Max was hanged for his crimes.

THE BLOOD LIBEL

Not far from our town of Bialystok was a small village. The prince who was the landlord there was a fine person. He dealt well with the Jews and the Jews, in turn, had an abundant livelihood. Not far from the village was an inn that belonged to the prince and was leased to a Jew. This Jew was a *ben-torah* (a religious scholar) and a *bal tzadik* (a righteous man), and was an excellent host. Jews had run the inn for generations. The innkeeper had married off his children, lived to see grandchildren, and thanked the Lord of the Universe for His mercy in dealing with them.

The peasants from the district held their "little Jew" (as they called him) in high esteem because he was always good to them. When the peasants had a quarrel among themselves, they came to the innkeeper to resolve the problem. He would also help them out from time to time with an interest-free loan, so the relationship between them was harmonious.

Then, one day, a calamity occurred. The town priest, who was a fine man, died. A new priest came to replace him, but as soon as he stepped foot in the community it was clear that he was an anti-Semite. In his Sunday sermons he poured fire and brimstone on the Jews and warned the peasants to have nothing to do with them, threatening the peasants with eternal Hell and the loss of the afterlife.

When the innkeeper found out what the priest was doing, he began to feel a bit uneasy. Who knew what (God forbid) might be the outcome of those sermons? However, he hoped and prayed that God would protect him and his family from evil.

When the priest realized that the peasants were not heeding his warnings and were continuing to deal with the Jews as they had before, he devised an evil scheme to take revenge on the Jews through the innkeeper.

In the area lived a peasant, a drunkard, who had no land of his own, only a hut far from town. He earned his living by hiring himself out to the local peasants. The priest befriended the drunkard and promised him both money and a reward in Heaven if he would do what he was told.

It happened that a poor widow with several children also lived in the district. This widow earned her livelihood from a small patch of land and a cow. One of her children was a boy of ten who would drive the cow to pasture there every day. The drunkard was to lure the boy to his hut and murder him there. Then, in the darkness of night, he was to conceal the victim in the cellar of the inn.

On the specified day, while the boy was in the pasture with the grazing cow, the drunkard approached him. With sweet words, he lured the child to his hut where he killed him. Then, according to plan, late that night he brought the boy's body to the inn, where he left it in the cellar.

When the boy did not return from the fields, the mother began to worry and inquired after him among her neighbors. When she couldn't find him, she went to the police and told them that her child had disappeared. The officer took several peasants and went back to the meadow to search for the boy, but there was no sign of him. When the officer returned from his search, the priest and the drunkard were already waiting for him. The mother fainted, and when she was revived, her shrieks reached up to the very heavens. The priest wasted no time, and immediately addressed the crowd that had gathered:

"Listen to what I have to tell you. The Jewish Easter is coming soon. They eat matzos. They must have Christian blood for the matzos. Clearly, the innkeeper has murdered this child and used his blood for the matzos."

The peasants were astonished at the priest's words. "Our little Jew a murderer? That can't be true. He is a good man and has helped all of us." "Very well," shouted the priest, "let us search the inn."

Because the inn was outside the village, the innkeeper didn't know what had happened. He was awakened by a loud knocking on the door. When he opened the door and saw the priest and the crowd of peasants, he became very frightened.

"What brings you here in the middle of the night, Little Father?"

The priest answered, "A little boy has disappeared. We have searched all over but found no sign of him, so we want to look here, too."

"You surely won't find him here, because I never set eyes on the boy."

The priest and the crowd of peasants rushed into the house like demons and searched every corner but couldn't find the youngster. The priest told the men to search the barn, but he wasn't there, either. When the peasants were just about ready to return to their homes, the priest told them to look in the cellar.

The men went down into the cellar and found a bloody sack. When they opened it, the hideous sight made them like madmen. Formerly good friends were suddenly transformed into wild animals, and they began to beat the Jew with deadly blows. The sheriff shouldered his way in and didn't allow them to continue, then arrested him.

The next morning a police official came and interrogated the innkeeper about the murdered child. The innkeeper swore he had never laid eyes on the child. "I've never in my life committed any crime, no less a murder. I swear by Eternal God that my hands are clean of any blood. Someone else killed the boy and wants the blame to fall on me."

"Listen to me," said the official, "I must take you away from here, because it isn't safe for you. I'll bring you to the city with me and will keep you in prison there until your trial. I assure you, if your innocence can be proven, you will be freed."

When the Jews of the city heard that a fellow Jew from a nearby district was charged with a blood libel, they lost no time in hiring a good lawyer and preparing for the trial.

Several weeks later, the sheriff noticed that the drunken peasant was wearing a pair of new boots, a new overcoat, and a hat with a shiny visor. He began to wonder how such an individual suddenly had the money to buy all these things. The sheriff began to get suspicious and decided to keep an eye on him. One day he was waiting for the peasant outside a tavern when the man left the place dead drunk. The sheriff followed him to his shack and began to question him. In his drunken state, the peasant blurted out the truth.

The sheriff immediately put shackles on his wrists and went with him to the priest. When the priest saw the peasant in chains, he became white as chalk. Then the sheriff told the priest he had come to arrest him because the peasant had confessed. The priest tried to lie, but it didn't help.

The sheriff brought both men to the city and there, under close examination, they both confessed. The Jew was immediately freed. The priest and the peasant were sentenced to life in prison at hard labor.

Isaac and Kayla Goldberg

IN THE NICK OF TIME

I would like to tell you about an unusual event that happened 45 years ago.

About 15 miles from Bialystok was a town that belonged to a rich landowner. He wasn't a bad person and conducted business with the local Jews, who made a few dollars from this.

Not far from the town was an inn that also belonged to the landowner. For many years it was rented to a Jew. The innkeeper was called Reb Shleyme, an unusual person among those townsfolk: a learned man and a hospitable person. The doors of Reb Shleyme's inn were always open for guests. Everyone knew that at Reb Shleyme's one would eat well, have a good place to sleep, and often a parting gift of a few rubles. In addition to the inn, Reb Shleyme carried on trade with the town; he was an honorable, rich man.

Reb Shleyme had a large family: sons, daughters and sons-in-law, and everyone lived together near the inn. Once a week Reb Shleyme would go into town to buy things needed for the inn.

Once, on a winter's Sabbath eve, after he had said the *havdole* prayer, Reb Shleyme decided to go to town to buy a few items. A Russian worked for the family from the time he was a youngster. He lived with them and was considered "one of the family." Reb Shleyme told Stashik (that was the Russian's name) to hitch the horses to the sleigh and get everything ready for the trip into town.

When Stashik left the house, Reb Shleyme took money from a locked cabinet, spread it out on the table, and started to tally the week's profits. When Stashik returned to tell his employer that everything was ready for the trip, he saw the money on the table, and hunger for the money ignited his lust. He stood near the table and looked at the money and dark thoughts began to work in his brain.

When Reb Shleyme finished counting the money, he tossed it into a sack, put on his warm fur coat with a woolen scarf around his throat and a fur hat. He took the sack of money and said, "Come on, Stashik." They both got into the sleigh, which had been bedded with straw. Stashik whipped the horses and they sped away at a gallop.

The night was a beautiful one; the moon shone in the middle of the sky and lighted the way. It was as bright as the middle of the day. Reb Shleyme felt appreciative of what was around him and thanked G-d that gave him a good living for the members of his household.

Suddenly, Stashik stopped the horses. The sleigh stood still. Reb Shleyme turns to Stashik: "What happened? Why did you stop the horses? Has something happened?"

"No, boss, nothing is wrong with the sleigh or with the horses. I've decided to kill you and take the sack of money."

Reb Shleyme laughed and said, "Surely, you're making a joke, Stashik. What's the matter with you? Have you gone crazy? Whip the horses and let's go on."

"I'm not joking. I really mean it. I want your money."

"If that's the case," said Reb Shleyme, "take the money and let's go back home."

By the light of the moon, he noticed that Stashik's eyes looked as if they were on fire, and Reb Shleyme realized that he was in great danger. To yell for help was useless; they were in the middle of the woods and there was no living soul to be seen.

He tried to talk to Stashik in a good way. "Just think about what you want to do. You want to murder me! I always treated you like my own child and gave you a good home; you were always a quiet, fine person and now suddenly you want to murder me, your protector! Think about how this is sinning against God. And until you die, your conscience will plague you. Your real punishment will first come to pass in the next world. You will burn in Hell. There they will burn your flesh; you will never have respite. I'm begging you, don't do this. If you want the money, take it. I promise that I will tell no one that you took my money."

"No, boss, I know that you will not keep quiet. You'll turn me over to the police and they'll send me off to hard labor. I have to kill you and take your money. I'll come home and say that we were attacked by robbers. They dragged you out of the sleigh and killed you and I ran away. No one will know who murdered you."

He then pulled a knife from the top of his boot and got ready to assault Reb Shleyme.

"Please, Stashik, let me at least say *vidui*. We Jews must say this prayer when we're at the point of death."

"All right, but hurry up. Somebody might come by."

Reb Shleyme began to say his prayer with a broken heart.

Then something strange happened. Stashik said to him, "If you want to save your life, take a rope out of the sleigh and tightly bind me hand and foot. Do it quickly before I change my mind."

Reb Shleyme immediately took the rope and bound Stashik. When Stashik was tightly bound, Reb Shleyme turned the sleigh around, whipped the horses, and arrived home, half dead from fright.

When the family heard the sleigh stop near the house, everyone ran out to see what had happened. They saw a very strange sight. Stashik was tied up like a calf being led to slaughter; he was struggling against the ropes and roaring like an ox.

Reb Shleyme looked at everyone with terrified eyes and could not utter a word. They brought him into the house until he calmed down. He told them what had happened and how he had a narrow escape from certain death thanks to a miracle from heaven.

Word spread through the town about what had occurred. The landowner came and had Stashik thrown into a dungeon overnight.

The next morning the landowner called the community leaders together. The first thing he ordered was that Stashik be given fifty lashes, and afterwards turned over to the police.

Stashik suffered through the fifty lashes with lips clenched against the pain, but uttered not a word. After this punishment was completed, the landowner told the leaders to call the police.

Stashik protested, "I'm not guilty; I'm no murderer. The Devil convinced me to do it!" He cried out to Reb Shleyme, "I couldn't resist the temptation when I saw the bag of money on your table. Then, when you started to pray, something touched my heart. I realized that I had to do something and told you to tie me up." Then Stashik hung his head and was silent.

Stashik's words touched Reb Shleyme and he said, "I believe that you were overwhelmed with lust for the money, and if the landowner agrees, I'll forgive you and you can come back home with me. You'll do your work as before because I believe that you've repented. I sense a real tone of regret in what you say."

The landowner was moved by Reb Shleyme's words. He couldn't believe that anyone could forgive such a crime and then bring the person back into his home. He agreed and left Stashik in Reb Shleyme's hands to deal with as he saw fit.

To the assembled crowd, the landowner said, "Now I understand why it is said that Jews are 'merciful sons of merciful fathers.' "

Stashik remained in Reb Shleyme's employ for many years, and even when Reb Shleyme passed away, Stashik continued to work for his family until he eventually died at a very old age.

A WONDERFUL BIALYSTOKER
SELF-DEFENSE ORGANIZATION IN 1906

A ll of us who came here to America in those years remember very well the pogrom when many of our landsmen died at the hands of the pogromists. Who among us can forget the long lines of dead bodies in the hospital courtyard? The ravaged corpses were silent witnesses to the terrible agonies that were inflicted on them, with the result that death was merciful when it freed them from their pain.

But I will not write about the pogrom. What I want to do is simply to tell of the work of the self-defense group and the difficult struggle that it had until it built the strength to stand up to the pogromists.

In the self-defense group were assembled all political parties and it was thanks to this organization that many Jewish lives were saved. Those were the times when the darkness of reactionism swirled over all Russia. Jewish blood ran like water. The Czarist government felt that it was losing the ground under its feet, so it resorted to the proven method of instigating pogroms against Jews. With the pogroms the government wanted to divert the attention of the population from the hopelessness of their pitiable condition. At that time pogroms swirled over all the settlements. Then the Jewish self-defense group appeared in the streets. And just as the pillar of flame lit the way for the Hebrews in the desert, so did the self-defense group illuminate the darkness of Jewish life at that time. The group aroused in each person the strength to defend his life. The fighting slogan was *"Tamoot nafshi im pleshteem."* (I shall die among the Philistines.) And just as we will never forget the heroes of the Bialystoker Ghetto [in World War II] who extracted payment for their murder, a life for a life, so also did the Bialystoker self-defense organization, many years earlier, show the way to defend against murder. For that reason we must never forget them.

Once the group was organized, the members were faced with a question: Where could they get arms? That a pogrom would take place in Bialystok was sure. That information came from the Jewish soldiers who served in Bialystok. At that time, a group of Poalei-Tzion members, the "Boyeveh" organization, held a meeting to find somehow a way to procure arms. They wrangled for a long time but were unable to reach a tangible solution. A restlessness became evident among those assembled. The situation was critical. No way became apparent to obtain money for arms. Then one of the members stood up and said: "Friends, I have been thinking about this for a long time and I have come to the conclusion that the only way to get arms is by expropriation." Everyone suddenly became silent. The atmosphere became tense. Something terrible lay in that word. And the comrade continued, "It is foolish to think that you will be able to gather funds through voluntary contributions. We'll have to get it ourselves. My plan is as follows: As you all know, I am an employee of Eli Melakh's office in Yatke Street. I know the time when a lot of money can be found in the cashbox. If you agree, I will bring you all the important details. With my help it will not be difficult to carry out this plan. I'm not fooling myself. I realize that this is a very risky undertaking. It might well cost some lives. I don't see any other solution. If you agree, I will immediately set to work. If we want the organization to have any substance, to have something with which to stand up to the pogromists, we don't dare wait because time does not stand still."

When the assemblage recovered from their surprise, it was decided after more long debates how to carry out the "expropriation." They immediately began to work out all the details. The date was agreed upon—the first of May—because on that day a substantial sum could be expected to be in the cashbox. It was decided to meet again in a few days.

By the second meeting we had already received a report with all the details. The participants went to work immediately and agreed upon what each one would do. The work was divided among those who would be responsible for getting in, those responsible for the telephone, and those whose responsibility was the cashbox. Every possible pitfall was anticipated to the smallest detail because even the smallest slip could cost lives.

As the time neared the agreed upon day, it was decided to have the last meeting at the Gorodoski Orchard. On the morning of May first everyone came together and once more went through all the steps. The final instructions were given. Everyone gave his word that if something went wrong, no one would betray anyone else's identity. One by one they left the orchard, each by a different path, in order not to attract any attention.

As the appointed hour struck, they headed toward the office from all different directions. Quickly each one took his post. Outside, life went on normally; no one suspected what was taking place inside the office. It didn't take long. The comrades left the office one by one. Each went in another direction, and in a very few minutes no trace was left of anyone.

It seemed as if everything went off perfectly. When they finally gathered together in the previously determined spot, however, it was discovered that one person was missing. Someone was immediately sent back to the office to see what had happened. Apparently, as soon as the "job" was done and the men left the office according to plan, one of the employees ran out into the street and began shouting that the cashbox had been stolen. People came running; there was great tumult because people thought that it was a pogrom.

The police quickly arrived, surrounded all the nearby streets, and began to search from house to house and from courtyard to courtyard. They found him in one of the courtyards. They searched him and found a loaded revolver and a substantial sum of money. Had the comrade followed the instructions not to stop anyplace but to go straight to the agreed upon rendezvous, he would never have been captured. However, he believed that since he had a large portion of the money, it would be safer if he waited until the tumult passed. Unfortunately, this was a fatal error. The police took him to prison. There they tortured him horribly to make him reveal the names of the others. He endured all the agonies but never betrayed anyone with so much as a single word.

Then there began a movement to free him from prison. They succeeded in bribing one of the guards who watches the prisoners when they exercise in the prison courtyard in order to get a bit of air. Outside, a *droshke* (carriage) was waiting. It looked like everything was going along better than expected. Unfortunately, at the last minute, something happened and the rescue fell through.

A little while later it was found out that he would be sent with a group of convicts to the city of Grodna. The group was supposed to leave on Friday at two o'clock in the morning. As the group passed by the Russian Orthodox Church, an assault was made on the convoy. Shooting occurred and in the confusion he escaped. However, he didn't get any further than Shmuel Shmid Street. There he was recaptured and returned to prison. A little while later, when he was in the Grodna prison, an alliance was formed with comrades from Grodna so that together they could free him. However, these combined efforts were unsuccessful. His sentence was to take place in Petersburg.

Several wealthy individuals from Bialystok took an interest in his situation because his father was employed by one of them. Good lawyers were hired, and individual Petersburg intercessors interested themselves in the case. But all the efforts were to no avail. He was sentenced to the gallows. There began to be some concerns among the upper classes. Certain Jews thought it best to keep still until an audience could be arranged with the Minister, and the Minister finally commuted the death sentence to hard labor.

Weeks and months he dragged himself over all Russia along with the worst criminals. In the group of convicts were the worst outcasts. One can imagine what he endured from them, but he comforted himself with the thought that soon he would arrive at the appointed place of his imprisonment and there would be an end to the wanderings. However, on route to one of the far-flung Russian provinces, the convicts attacked the convoy and shooting broke out. A bullet found him and he fell dead.

This sad story I will never forget until my last breath. Dear comrade Avraham Moshe! May your memory be recalled together with all the freedom fighters who sacrificed their young lives on the altar of freedom. Blessed be your memory.

Translator's Note

Several years later, after he had come to America, the writer married. His first-born son, my brother, was named Avraham Moshe after his beloved friend.

Until this story was translated, no one in the family was aware of these events. My brother himself didn't know the story of his namesake.

A Further Expansion from the
Bialystoker Memorial Book, 1982
by David Sohn

"The Jewish Self-Defense League played an important role in saving Jews during those pogrom days. The league was organized by the labor parties. It saved thousands of Jewish lives and a great deal of their property. Thanks to this defense league, several major Jewish working-class sections of the city were spared ruination. As soon as the pogrom began, a company of soldiers on horses eagerly rode into these areas with the intent of razing them to the ground. But before they could enter, a Jewish anarchist tossed a grenade that exploded with a fierce impact, smashing many windows and devastating the surrounding houses. The horses panicked and their riders rode away. From then on, not one of the soldiers or police officers dared come near those streets.

At every corner of the poor section of Bialystok, patrols of the Jewish Self-Defense League were stationed with revolvers and grenades, each group under one leader. They guarded the streets and fired warning shots into the air. If a gentile went by carrying loot, these Jewish protectors would frighten him until he threw down the stolen package and fled. The stolen items were gathered together and later brought to a central location. Many more tragedies would have occurred had it not been for these self-defense groups."

A RUINED HOLIDAY

Every year, after Yom Kippur, all the neighbors would come together in our courtyard to fulfill the *mitzvah* (good deed) of hammering a pole into the earth, the beginning of a new *sukkah* (a tabernacle built of wood and branches ouside Jewish homes for the *Sukkos* (harvest holiday) After honoring this *mitzvah,* the neighbors would gather in our home, sit around the table, and begin to plan the *sukkah.*

Every year the *sukkah* was built in a corner between two houses. The logic was simple, because this way only two walls needed to be added. Since there were few materials with which to build the *sukkah,* using the two existing walls meant saving building materials. The architect was my father. All the residents assumed responsibility for bringing materials: a window shutter, a door, a board. A piece of metal was also useful.

When they had finished planning the *sukkah,* my mother would serve tea and cake that she had baked before Yom Kippur. As they were drinking tea, the men would talk about the cantors and Torah readers who had prayed in the synagogues. They talked about those who had prayed properly and well and those who had not. After finishing the tea, they would go home until the next day when they would begin to build the *sukkah.*

The next morning after prayers, the courtyard was as busy as a beehive. Jews in skullcaps ran hither and yon. One was carrying a board, another a shutter from a window, and someone else a long board used in making noodles. When all the materials that could be found were amassed, they started to build the *sukkah*.

First of all, we youngsters were honored with the task of pulling out any nails and straightening them so that they could be used for the *sukkah*. I will never forget how proud we were that we were included in the group of *sukkah* builders. Who cared that we banged our fingers as long as we, too, participated in the big *mitzvah!*

When everything was ready, the men got to work. They put together a piece of metal and a piece of wood, a shutter and a noodle board, each person suggesting a solution as to where to nail together the board and the shutter or the piece of metal. My father, the architect, ignored all the advice.

Everyone happily dragged and climbed and was proud of the *mitzvah* of building a *sukkah*. When the *sukkah* was almost finished, it was noticed that there was no wood left to make a door. My father didn't despair. "Don't worry, neighbors, where does it state that a *sukkah* must have a wooden door? We will hang up a blanket and it will serve very nicely as a door."

Later, my father, along with another Jew, went outside of town to wait for a Christian couple who were bringing fir branches for the roof of the *sukkah*. After finishing the transaction, they brought the boughs home and began to put the roof on the *sukkah*. My father climbed a ladder and some men handed up the boughs. Others went inside the *sukkah*. With long sticks they poked through the roof to show where additional matting was needed until the roof was covered according to proper custom.

When they were finished building, they turned jurisdiction over to the women so they could decorate the inside of the *sukkah*. The women hung sheets and tablecloths on the walls. They hung various fruits from the rafters: apples, pears and grapes. They poured yellow sand on the earthen floor and the *sukkah* was finished. The only thing left was to bring in tables and chairs. But this had to wait until the eve of *Sukkot* (harvest holiday) Now everyone asked The One Above for good weather so they could eat in the *sukkah*.

On the eve of *Sukkos,* the men went to synagogue for the *Ma'ariv* prayer. The women brought their candles into the *sukkah* and said the holiday blessing over them. When the men returned from synagogue, they went into the *sukkah* to make *kiddush* (a blessing over wine) (each hoped that his *kiddush* would be the best) and then to eat the holiday feast. The women brought in the delicious-smelling holiday delicacies: gefilte fish, noodle soup, and *tzimis* (a meat and vegetable stew). After the meal, the men prayed in a *minyan (a prayer group of ten men)* and then everyone went home to sleep.

While the residents were blissfully asleep under their quilts, a tragedy was taking place in the courtyard. Our landlord had a mischievous nanny goat. She had to be kept locked in her stall because she used to do a great deal of damage. However, that night, someone forgot to lock her up, and when everything was quiet, the goat got out of her stall and wandered around the courtyard. Her nostrils must have been filled with the smell of fresh fir boughs, so she apparently decided that she must sample the greenery to see how it tasted. She climbed up on the *sukkah*, made herself comfortable on the roof, and began to chew the boughs. The rafters that supported the boughs revolted, and both the roof and the goat fell and the *sukkah* was destroyed.

When folks woke up the next morning and saw the destruction, everyone was broken hearted. The final result was that we had to eat on both days of the holiday in a neighboring courtyard's *sukkah* and the women, unfortunately, had to carry all the food over the fence. The holiday was ruined by a mischievous goat.

Epilogue
Bialystok – A Historical Survey

BY I. SHMULEWITZ

The Jewish community in Bialystok, which achieved so much on all fronts, goes back some 500 years. Its story is fascinating and unique. Until World War II, Jewish Bialystok was renowned in Russia, Poland and other countries as a center of commerce and industry. It was also celebrated for its Torah learning and charity, a broad network of cultural and community activities, labor, art and industry.

To understand Bialystok is to appreciate the enterprising spirit of its Jews, as well as their boundless capacity for compassion— helping the helpless, comforting the downtrodden, sustaining the impoverished. Above all, Jewish life and thought in Bialystok were diversified; many different points of view were held concerning all the important issues of the day. Bialystok was a place for people to grow and thrive, to face challenges and overcome adversity. This community accommodated multiple economic classes, social strata, political parties and theological positions.

Living in freedom was the major goal of Jews in Bialystok from all walks of life. No one held a monopoly on truth, ideas or values. The environment bubbled like a cauldron into which ingredients of all kinds were thrown.

There was a sense of community among Bialystok's Jewish inhabitants. They all felt they belonged to one another. If the ugly head of alienation appeared from time to time, it did not endure for long. For there existed an intricate network of aid institutions, whether organized or informal, reaching out to those on the fringes of society.

As we will soon see, the very emergence of Bialystok from a barren, uncultivated swampland in the forests of Eastern Poland into a flourishing, sprawling center of human life was a tribute to the creativity, industriousness and hard work of its Jews. Let us go back in time and briefly review some milestones in its evolution.

Around the 10th century CE, the Bialystok region was populated by a barbaric Baltic-Latvian tribe. Subsequently, its members were expelled from the area by Russian-Lithuanian conquerors. In 1320, Bialystok was founded as a village by the Lithuanian Count Gedimin. After being passed on from one generation of this Lithuanian family to the next, the village became the private fiefdom of King Zygmunt August, a Polish ruler, in 1542.

At the end of the 16th century, the Arians, a heretical Christian cult that did not accept several major Catholic dogmas, occupied Lithuania and Poland. They invaded a temple in Bialystok built many years before-hand and "defiled" it. These apostates were driven out, and in 1668 Bialystok went on to become an entrenched Polish territory. In 1795, following the partition of Poland, Prussia annexed Bialystok. Napoleonic armies on their way to Russia took over control of Bialystok and ruled for one year. Then in 1808, the city fell into Russian hands. Napoleon reconquered Lithuania and Poland in 1812, and three years later, after the Tilsit Peace Conference, Russia once again imposed its jurisdiction over the city, ruling for more than a century—until the first World War. Poland took over in 1919 until the outbreak of World War II in 1939, when for two years the Russians controlled Bialystok. The Nazis captured the city in 1941 and destroyed it in 1943.

The above reflects a history of political and social instability in Bialystok for almost 1,000 years. This town was a veritable football, kicked back and forth, first between groups and then nations vying with one another for dominance in the area. Under these conditions of flux and uncertainty, it is all the more amazing that Bialystoker Jews found it possible to grow, to build, to establish security and continuity through the many institutions they established.

Documents in Tyktin, the original capital city of the region, show that Jews already lived in Bialystok around 1658. In 1703, Polish Count Jan Klements Bronicki built for himself a wooden palace in Bialystok. The old Bet Hamidrash was constructed in 1718 within what was to be known as the synagogue court. In 1742, Bronicki elevated the village of Bialystok to the status of a city. Jews were granted equal rights in 1745. In that same year, Bronicki erected a tower that served as a detention center for criminals. At the base of this tower eighty shops were constructed, which Bronicki allocated for Jewish businessmen.

*Germans hand over Bialystok to the Soviets
on September 22, 1939.*

Bialystok, located near the Bialy River (Bialystok means "White River" in Polish), became a haven for Jews. Bronicki invited them to settle there and build up the town; he provided them with land, lumber and other materials. In 1749 a small number of Jews settled in Bialystok, totaling 765 by 1765. In the next fifty years the Jewish community grew in both numbers and influence. In 1800 the "new *Bet Hamidrash*" was established in the synagogue court. Bialystok replaced Tyktin as the dominant city, surrounded by smaller satellite communities such as Choroscz, Horodok, Janowa, Jaszynowka, Knyszin, Odelsk, Sokola, Zabludowa, and Waszlykowa.

Rabbi Aron Halewi Horowic opened the first print shop in

Bialystok in 1804. In 1807, about 6,000 inhabitants lived in the city, 4,000 of them Jews. Bialystok was declared the capital of the region in 1808. By 1897, 42,000 inhabited Bialystok, the Jews constituting 64 percent of the population.

Thus, from the Jewish community's inception until its brutal liquidation by the Nazis, the Jews played a major role in the life of Bialystok. But there were frequent ups and downs. At times they enjoyed prosperity, as well as periods of relative well-being and security. At other times, repeated political and economic crises plagued them, forcing some Jews to flee Bialystok for other countries. This trend reached its peak in the 1880s and 1890s, when Bialystoker Jews arrived in the United States, Argentina, Israel and other lands. Wherever they settled, however, they brought with them the pride of their origin. They transplanted their civic spirit, their zest for living, their creativity and their ingenuity to their new homes.

Shortly before 1914, 80 percent of Bialystok's inhabitants were Jews. Virtually its entire economic and social infrastructure was in Jewish hands. By 1939, just before the Nazi invasion of Poland, 100,000 people lived in Bialystok, 60,000 of them Jews. The ethnic mixture of the city included Poles, Jews, Russians, White Russians, Germans and Lithuanians.

THE JEWISH COMMUNITY

Jewish Bialystok was well known throughout Russia, Lithuania, Poland and other places as a center of Jewish culture, variegated social activities and philanthropy. It always joined other major Jewish communities in Eastern Europe in assisting needy Jews with generosity and enthusiasm. The town was the cradle of the *Chovevei Zion* (Lovers of Zion) movement. This focus on Israel as the Jewish homeland was sharpened when, in 1882, several prominent Bialystoker pioneers helped establish Petach Tikvah in Israel. They founded businesses, built houses, and organized cultural and social institutions in the Holy Land.

Israel was, however, not the only part of the world in which Bialystoker Jews invested their energy and resources. Mosesville, a Jewish colony in Argentina, was formed through the efforts of Jewish Bialystok. Villa Lynch, an industrial center in Argentina, came into being as a result of the initiative, efforts and money of Jews in Bialystok.

In the United States, Mexico, South America, Western Europe and Israel, there are today significant communities of Bialystoker landsleit to whom perpetuating the heritage of their beloved hometown is essential. We shall see later on in greater detail the contributions of Bialystokers to various lands.

Needless to say, the Jewish citizens of Bialystok did not neglect their hometown itself. They organized Yiddish- and Hebrew-speaking schools, gymnasiums (advanced high schools), libraries, theaters, music groups, sports clubs, and a multiplicity of other cultural organizations. Habimah, the famous Hebrew theater company that has delighted audiences throughout the world, was started by Nochum Cemach, a Bialystoker Jew.

The city had an intelligentsia that included writers, scientists, actors, musicians, artists, educators and political leaders. In the religious sphere, Bialystok produced great rabbis, Talmudists and yeshiva educators who spiritually uplifted the Jewish community. They functioned within more than one hundred synagogues and yeshivot in the city and its environs and encouraged the masses to maintain contact with their Jewish tradition—to study and pray. Generations of Jewish children were educated in these institutions. Young students from nearby towns came to Bialystok to study Torah in its highly regarded yeshivot. Their hosts, among the most gracious, generous and hospitable Jewish families to be found in Eastern Europe, provided them with food and lodging.

One of the distinguishing features of the Jewish community in Bialystok was its absolute dedication to assisting the poor. The community established its own Jewish hospital, a *Linas Hatzedek* (a free clinic where physicians donated their services to the destitute and medications were dispensed gratis), an old age home, orphanages, aid societies and lending institutions. Many individuals, both men and women, felt an obligation to serve as alms collectors. They solicited donations from the Jewish population and then distributed the funds to the needy. The poor were also provided with wood and coal for heat, food for the Jewish holidays, money to help pay their rent, and marriage dowries for their daughters. All of this was done quietly and with the greatest discretion to preserve the dignity of the recipients.

The Jewish community of Bialystok displayed the best traits of the Jewish people as a whole: ambition mixed with mercy. It left a record of rich and ennobling achievements. There was every reason to expect that many more pages would be added to the chronicle, which would have made it even more impressive, had Bialystok continued to exist.

Unhappily, the Nazi juggernaut, in its diabolical effort to annihilate every Jew, did not spare this illustrious center of Jewish creativity and compassion. The town was utterly destroyed, but its legacy must never be forgotten.

This *Bialystok Memorial Book,* therefore, represents the last and best attempt of *landsleit* who remember Jewish Bialystok to make certain that the legacy outlined in this chapter will long be remembered. Future generations, it is hoped, will sift through these pages and discover their roots, physically buried under the rubble but spiritually everlasting.

The tragedy of Bialystok's destruction was eloquently described in a poem written by Z. Segalowicz, titled "My Bialystok." He likens his memories of his beloved hometown to a book that has fallen into a fire, consumed by the hungry flames. Disbelieving and catapulted into a state of shock, the poet asks, "What happened to my town? My generation? My past? Where are my family and friends? How devastating it was for an entire breed of believers with high hopes and expectations, bubbling with pride, filled with courage and awaiting a bright future, to be condemned to oblivion by a raving and bloodthirsty nation." Surely all we can do is to rewrite, though in abridged form, the original book incinerated in the fire.

The epilogue is from *The Bialystoker Memorial Book – Der Bialystoker Yizkor Buch,* the Bialystoker Center, New York 1982. © copyright by the Bialystoker Center and I. Shmulewitz. Reprinted with Permission from Aaron Shmulewitz.

I. (Icek) Shmulewitz (1911-1986) was a Yiddish journalist, writer and lecturer in Paris and New York, who wrote primarily in the *Jewish Daily Forward,* mostly about the Holocaust, and the lives that its survivors rebuilt after the war. He was born in Kielce, Poland.

NOTES ON SOURCES

1. All the stories in Tales of Bialystok were written by Charles Zachariah Goldberg and published in "Der Amerikaner" *(The American Newspaper)* in Yiddish and also in the *Bialystoker Shtime (The Bialystoker Voice)* in the 1930s and 1940s.

2. Many photos are used with permission of Tomasz Wisniewski whose book *Jewish Bialystok and Surroundings in Eastern Poland: A Guide for Yesterday and Today* is a seminal work in research and documentation in preserving the history of the Jewish people in Bialystok and what is now eastern Poland.

3. All other photos are taken from the long-out-of print *Bialystok— Photo Album of a Renowned City and Its Jews The World Over* by David Sohn. All reasonable attempts were made to find copyrights for these photos.

4. One other book we recommend highly is *Jewish Bialystok and Its Diaspora (The Modern Jewish Experience)* by Rebecca Kobrin.

CPSIA information can be obtained
at www.ICGtesting.com
Printed in the USA
BVHW04s0156090418
512833BV00016B/337/P